"NANOBUGGED" IS THE TRUE ACCOUNTS OF HOW A SMALL TOWN YOUNG MAN BECAME UNWILLINGLY INVOLVED WITH THE DEA, FBI, AND CIA. THE YOUNG MAN, "SHEP" SET HIMSELF UP FOR THE WRATH OF A GANG OF RENEGADE FEDERAL AGENTS AND FOUND IT TO BE AN OVERWHELMING SITUATION. THE EVENTS THAT LED TO THE IDEA AND THE REALNESS OF POSSIBLY BEING A HUMAN BUG (A HUMAN WALKIE-TALKIE) BECAME CONVINCING ENOUGH. HE HAD TWO CHOICES, LET IT KILL HIM OR TURN THE WRATH TO GRAPES. SEEING THE AMPLIFICATION OF HIS SITUATION GAVE VIEW TO THE DIRECTION ALL MANKIND IS BOUND IN. SO GRAPES IT WOULD BE.

ALL THIS RUNS TOGETHER ON RAILS OF TRUTH. DELIVERING THE READER TO THE FINAL CHAPTER, AND THAT IS WHEN THE PURPOSE OF THE BOOK HAS ONLY JUST BEGAN.

Chapter *1*

The cool concrete flooring of the screen porch on the front of the light green cement block house was highly contrasted by the hot tin roof.

Kicking her legs, sitting in the front porch swing was Reba, 20, long brown hair, but not too fluffy, large brown eyes, and a beautifully balanced body nothing too big, nothing too small. She looked so pretty and soft wearing blue jean shorts, pink tank top, and just enough smile to show off her dimples.

Shep, a "Mel Gibson, of the first Mad Max movie," looking young man of 27, sat in a rocking chair, pulling the strings of his just below the knees cut off shorts, rock'n an AC/DC t-shirt.

They had their one night stands years ago, but them day's were gone. She was shacked up with his cousin now. His cousin Deryl was a handsome brown haired, blue eyed, 26 year old, of medium build.

Reba swept the bangs from her eyes and turned up a bottle of Bud Light. Looking at the floor she said "Ya' know ya' ain't goanna have shit if ya' don't stop smoking crack."

Shep stopped staring at her and gazed at the pecan trees in the front yard. "When I get back from the mountains, I ain't goanna' smoke it any more." He wanted to believe that this rehab would do the trick, but he knew full well the power of the jones. Stopping seemed impossible.

Unless…maybe he was right about his 6 year quest to figure out the manufacturing process of methamphetamine. He had done meth for two years. This was before he started smoking crack. The meth supply had been cut off, and foolishly he tried crack and ended up hooked on something he hated for four years.

The production process was known to few around these parts in those days, and thought to be out of reach of the common man. Picking up info from chemistry books and rumors and Georgia Public Television he was sure he had it. The chemicals availability was stopping him. That and the fact that he wanted crack so bad he couldn't buy the first box of cold pills. The crack was so MORE, MORE, MORE.

Reba cut her eyes his way. "Ya' reckon it's going to be that easy to kick it?"

"Hell no, I wanna' take this five bucks in my pocket down to Black Bottom and try to get a dime rock with it."

In the middle of a swallow of ice cold Bud she brought down the bottle, trying not to laugh, spraying beer all over the porch. "Damn it Shep, now you done made me waste some good beer."

Shep stood up and fished the five dollar bill from his pocket and dropped it in her lap. "Here have this before I do something stupid with it, and let me get one of them cold ones."

"Help yourself, Oh, well lookee' there it's Gabby."

The caming out of the 50's model truck came steady up the asphalt driveway as Shep headed to the fridge and open the back door, the entrance that everybody used. Going into the small kitchen he grabbed a cold one. She had them in the freezer for a little while so they were extra cold.

Gabby, a tuff built, 28 year old dude with medium length blond hair came through the back door, leaving it open. "What the hell's going on in here?"

"I'm enjoying my last day in Dry Branch, Georgia with my cuzzes' pretty girlfriend. Headed to rehab tomorrow."

Gabby reached in the fridge and grabbed a beer. Before the frig shut Reba hollered "I heard them bottles and you ain't drinking all my beer Gabby."

"No ma'am, I left you one." He winked at Shep there were three left.

"Killing me" she said, then with no worry really at all "O hell my masters home."

At the same time Shep and Gabby confirmed their innocents. "I just got here." They smiled at each other and toasted beer.

Reba followed suit "Ya' God damn right y'all did!"

Deryl's work van pulled up to the back door. He came clumping in the house with his work boots untied, wearing jeans and as always a blue Dickeys work shirt, sporting his name over the pocket. "What's up?"

Gabby caught him up "We just got here."

Deryl shook his head with a smirk, "hhu" he grunted.

Gabby spoke up quickly as he went out the back door. "I need you to check this capacitor for me. I ain't got my fluke."

"I thought you said you burnt your fluke up." Deryl said as they all three headed to Gabby's truck.

"I did, that's why I ain't got it with me."

They stood in the summer sun around the back of the truck testing capacitors and discussing air conditioning trouble shooting tactics. Shep just listened and learned. He loved to learn about all kinds of stuff. He had been doing electrical work, production line machinery, mechanical, and framing houses, sometimes this and some times that since age 18. Chemistry, quantum physics, and anything else was of interest.

Deryl finally spoke up. "What you doing Taiter head?" his nick name for Shep.

"Going to rehab tomorrow, in the north Georgia mountains."

Deryl's eyes exuberantly opened wide. "Bout' time, who's taking you?"

"My sister"

"Aww, little sister going to take care of big brother?"

"Anything to get rid of me."

Deryl tossed the capacitor over to Gabby and rolled the leads of his meter up. "It ain't no good Gabby."

Gabby put a can of Skoal in his back pocket and spit. "Reckon not."

Deryl propped his foot on the back bumper of the truck. "I might be leaving the country soon y'all."

Shep and Gabby just looked at him for more.

He obliged. "Russia"

He was getting the same look for more from Gabby and Shep.

"My brother Andy's high security clearance out at the Air Force base got me an application to do maintenance work at the U.S. Embassy."

Gabby kept a serious face. "If I get my fluke fixed ya' reckon I could get in on some of that?"

Deryl laughed and suddenly stopped with a, "No"

Gabby opened his truck door and bid his farewell to Reba, who was still sitting on the porch. "By Reba, thanks for the beer!"

A giggle came from the porch.

Shep opened the passenger door. "Drop me off at Gailu dr."

"Gailu dr.? It is all the way to the bottom of the hill."

The street of midclass brick houses was built by Shep and Deryl's Granddad and is only a stones throw away.

At the end of the driveway Gabby asked Shep "Hey man ya' know that shit ya' was wanting to make…?"

Shep interrupted, "Destiny sweet destiny. Yea but don't thank me thank Hitler."

With curiosity Gabby smiled "Hitler?"

"Yea GPTV had a documentary about him day before yesterday. I had figured it out but wasn't sure if I was right, till they gave me enough info to…. What I'm trying to say is I would put all my eggs in this basket."

Gabby grabbed a pen and note pad from over the visor. "Continue"

"OK how easy can you get some anhydrous ammonia from that place you work at?"

Gabby put the truck in park and wrote, anhydrous. "Oh, bout' as easy as the sun sets."

"Well, get ya' some of that and get ya' some………………."

Chapter 2

"Shep what's your drug of choice?" Says a grey headed white man with thick rimmed glasses.

Standing in front of a big two story white house. Shep could hear the clear as glass water of the Chattahoochee creek run its course over the flat bed of rocks. The only thing separating the house and the creek is the old country mountain highway, a bar that rented inter tubes for creek rides and beside that is a few picnic tables in a clearing on the creek bank.

"LSD is my drug of choice, but I have a problem with leaving crack cocaine alone."

The man rolled his eyes up & down with a brief smile, as if he was about to say something he'd said a million, and now one more time. "So you don't see LSD as a problem?"

"Yes, I love it. The problem is I only come across it an average of once a year."

"Well you're addicted to getting high. This is Narcotics Anonymous, a twelve step program." He folded his arms and slightly leaned forward toward Shep. "You do realize once an addict, always an addict?"

Shep turned and started walking toward the picnic area and the creek, leaving the man standing in front of the rehab house. With a smile he answered the man. "Well, I guess I better find me something better to be addicted to." He was glad he came to the mountains. It was a great place to free his mind.

The house was pretty cool. For two weeks there was no leaving the house. Shep would go to the bank of the water and wet his hair and face with the ice cold water. Meditating on the good things in his life.

There were six other young men living in the rehab house, until one left, quit, the same weekend Shep reached his two weeks. This opened up a job with a local contractor by the name of Brian Nelson, who also was the former Police and Fire Chief in the area.

The work was perfect. He would help the framer, the electrician, and the A/C man, who was also the roofer. Shep enjoyed the work; it was right up his alley. The men he worked with were cool.

A month went by, Shep didn't care for the 12 step program. He had to attend the house meetings twice a day after work. His paycheck went to rent and food then he got anything that was left over, which wasn't much. He got his kicks from reading L. Ron Hubbard's, <u>DIANETICS</u> and a book of Buddhist monk parables, <u>POINTING AT THE MOON</u>.

What happened was, one weekend after a month or so at the rehab house, Shep was helping the A/C man and the electrician install a heating system in the bar across the street from the rehab house. The nights were getting rather cool and the place had decided to try staying opened longer into the fall months.

They were installing the heat and the lil' cute, petite bar tender and Shep were playing eye tag. After her shift ended she saddled a bar stool and a bomb shell blond joined her for drinks. Shell and Marylin took a liking to Shep and likewise.

The cute one, Shell and her roommate Marylin had a two bed room brick house in a cow field just a few miles from town. Marylin snatched Shep's heart clean out of him and that very night he went to the rehab house and packed his belongings, and off to Shell's he went to move in with Marylin.

The guys at work already new Shep's new friends and the electrician came and picked him up from his new home every morning for work. The electrician and he hit it off well, both being into philosophy and science and etc..

Marylin and Shep had plenty of laughs and made a lot of love. She was hotter than a two dollar pistol, in more ways than one. Shell acted like the whole affair didn't bother her, but Shep could sense the let down she felt, after all she had made first contact.

Give the Devil his due, about 2 months before Christmas Marylin took Shep's heart and without warning, she even wore a smile, when she dropped it into a blender and grinded it to oblivion. Seems the ol' girl from Habersham County had an alternate life she had to get back to. She was gone with as little as a by.

Instead of doing what he should have done (Hind sites 20/20) and gave Shell what she was begging for by this point, he tucked his tail and had his ride back to Dry Branch on the way the same morning of Marylin's departure.

Chapter 3

Shep was looking out the back seat passenger window of the Nissan Maxima, which smelled like home, the mountains and valleys he was leaving behind rushed by.

The driver Deseray, brunet, always made Shep think of Mary Tyler Moore, was the girl friend of Shaky. Shaky, called that because of his constant nervous edge, sat beside her sipping on a beer looking like Toby

Keith. He and Shep understood each other, so there friendship from their teen years was still tight as ever.

Shaky turned and looked at Shep "Ya' want a cold one just pull that knob on the seat beside ya' and you can gain access to the cooler in the trunk."

"Naw man, lil' to early for me this time."

Deseray looked in the windshield rear view mirror, eyes to eyes with Shep "Ya' goanna stop smoking that shit?"

"I hope so."

Shaky let the seat up and a little bit "Enough room back there?" he asked.

"Yeah, plenty."

With the hesitation of a man that was scared of the answer, Shaky manned up and asked "Where ya' goanna live?"

Shep noticed the hesitation and couldn't blame him. He knew the troubles of taking on an unemployed, ride less, room renter, and wouldn't burden a friend like that. Maybe family, but not a friend. "I'm goanna stay with my Mom and Dad for as long as we can stand it."

Shaky chuckled, "You know I had to ask."

That got a smile from Deseray. "Shaky ain't committing to a damn thing, unless he has to, you know that."

"I appreciate the ask."

Deseray continued talking "I heard you was a working mountain man, who did you work for?"

"A man named Brian Nelson," Shep went on to explain his trip to rehab.

Shaky had a good job doing maintenance at a world wide tile plant, and Deseray was a nurse at a chiropractic office. The chit chat went on down the line. Every mile as they got closer, Shep's doubt of staying off crack grew stronger. Deseray saw the concern; she tried to put better thoughts into his head. "So I bet you're ready to see your son. He looks just like an 8 year old you, and his mama looks just like she did in high school. Well, close to it anyway with 3 young'uns under her belt. She still has the blonde hair, blue eyes, and she's still short. I can't believe she married Shane's lanky ass, but you did cheat on her, and she was your wife…"

Shep interrupted her, "Yeah, I'm ready to see Marcus. I've missed so much time with him in the last 6,7, well honestly I guess, all of it. Tiffany says she wants him to live with me. He & Shane aren't getting along, but I think Marcus has got a text book case of, You ain't my daddy."

Ain't no signs to welcome folks to Dry Branch, GA.. All of a sudden there ya' are. As they came East on Highway 80 they passed Deryl's green block house, pecan trees in the front yard and tin roof. Shep got excited, "Hold up, spin this thing around and drop me off at my cuz's."

Deseray went on down the hill to Gailu Dr. where she was headed to drop Shep off, and started to turn around. Shep opened the door to save her the trouble, "I appreciate the ride y'all. Just knowing I have friends like y'all means a lot. I love y'all!"

Shaky said "We love you too man, come see us."

With an, "Aww, ain't that sweet" from Deseray. This made Shep and Shaky both blush.

Shep hiked back up Highway 80 to Deryl's where he had seen Gabby's truck. Shep got to thinking, the subject never came up and if anything had come out of the recipe he gave Gabby, surely Shaky would have spilled the beans. With that in mind his hopes weren't very high.

Startling Gabby, he leaned up against the truck beside him, whose attention was staring at the back yard, consisting of Deryl's work van, and three sheds. "What's up, did you miss me?"

"Boy don't sneak up on me like that!"

It was then the pungent odor hit Shep's nose "Great time a' day! Ammonia, you worked it out?"

"Damn skippy, see that meat smoker out there," he motioned toward the middle of the back yard, and there surrounded by the sheds, house, and Deryl's white work van sat a meat smoker with a boat paddle leaning against it. "in that there smoker is a 5 gallon bucket with 3 ounces of the best speed I ever done in my life, cooking in it."

"Well, ya' need to let me try it when it gets done, I been jonesing for a crack rock since I left the mountains."

"Stick with me, and you'll never smoke crack again," Gabby was right, Shep would have a jones for crack for the next year and a half, but with the meth to take the edge off he broke the chains of something he had hated from the first time he tried it. He rode out the crack dreams, sometimes so real; it was reality but only a dream, if that makes sense. He rode out the pressure of his environment. Just being close to an area where he used to buy crack gave him bubble guts. The endless supply of meth he now had kept him from going down that road.

The impact of Shep giving Gabby that recipe would have on the future was more than imaginable. The "geeking craze" took off like a wild fire being fed by high winds. Gabby didn't know the importance of keeping his new found hobby a secret. He had showed others the science of it all, and those few showed more and more.

Chapter 4

Not all had the guts to cook meth, but there was more than enough cooks to supply the wants and needs. The crack heads, the soon to be crack heads, if meth hadn't stepped in, the rednecks, the city slickers, lawyers, cops, and right on round to the judges daughter. Shep seen them all buying it.

The paper man was the one to see this thing take off like nobody else. The route is delivered before daybreak in most areas. The amount of lights on in houses, where once sat nothing but darkness, was more noticeable. Being an extra amount of cars in the driveway too.

Shep didn't last long at his parent's house, after returning from the mountains. The nights of acting as if he was asleep seemed like such a waste of time. He landed a job, at an industrial pressure washing business. He talked Deryl into letting him move in, since Reba had kicked rocks, and Gabby was already staying there, Deryl figured, "What the hell, might as well."

More and more crack heads, the Caucasian ones, came to know meth as anti-crack and it worked. The meth did not affect, or maybe I should say infect, everyone the same. Some used it as a stepping-stone to get out of stronger addictions. To some it was just another chapter in their encyclopedia of ways to self-destruct. It was a fad, it was sad, it was the light, it was the fright. It brought skeletons out of the closet, it gained life long dependants. It saved, it killed, a parents nightmare, a parents divorce, a marriage.

The media put on its best scare tactics, only feeding the frenzy. What most didn't know, what they faild to do in all the hype of it all was to tell the truth, even to their selves. Methamphetamine unlike other drugs is only as addictive as you make it, but the drug it self is only as addictive as a cup of coffee for some, or a t-ball game in the yard with the kids could produce the same effect, or parachuting out an airplane. Like I said, more for some than others. I ain't promoting it. It is going to drag you down in the end I pretty much guarantee that, and it is illegal. It ain't crack or heroin or opiate based pills, more, more, more, more. If ya' on meth I'd suggest ya' stop, go to a t-ball game or jump from a plane it's legal and a lot more fun. If ya' smoke crack or a heroin junky or a pill popper, it can be stopped, and good luck with all that.

The chemicals in our bodies are shape like keys in a way. They only unlock certain receptors. Methamphetamine is shape like adrenaline. Meth takes longer to break down so it sticks to your ribs, on account of a carbon-to-carbon bond as opposed to a carbon to hydrogen bond in adrenaline.

More cooks came into the picture. The light green block house on Highway 80 in Dry Branch, Georgia became known as Sanford Arms. Sanford and Son was for the geek projects of junk that had accumulated in and around the sheds. Steadily being added to with all the horse-trading. The arms as the motel of checking in and out.

Shep was car-pooling with a DEA Special Agent's brother. The agent and his younger brother are a few years Shep's and Deryl's elder. They all grew up on the same "70's Show" street Gailu dr. With around thirty three other kids, teens, and young adults.

The DEA agent looks like Sonny Bono with a thickness to him. Coincidently from the mountains Shep had just left, his name is Brian Sterling Wilson, Sterling for short. As opposed to his ex-boss, named Brian Nelson.

Shep's ride to work, the agents brother, we'll call Sonny, was a stretched tall skinny version of Sonny Bono. He was an old school pothead. Been selling and smoking pot since the mid 70's.

The four-wheel drive tires on the black Toyota truck hummed down slower as Sonny turned into the liquor store. Sonny parked and opened his door "I'll be back." as he slid out the truck. He slipped off behind the liquor store.

Shep knew what it was, crack, and on his first day on the way home from work at his new job. As the tires sang that increasing high pitched whale leaving the liquor store Shep got them bubble guts. The nervousness of that rush to come like only crack can give. It had been around forty days since he had left the mountains and was all of a sudden wishing he could be back in Marylin's arms.

Sonny spoke up "Cat's out the bag now man. I'm goanna need to hit this at Deryl's. Ain't no way I can go home with it, the wife knows when I'm fucked up on it. I can't function, I get stuck and can't talk ya' know how it dose us."

Shep knew and couldn't blame Sonny for not going home to the ol' lady. She was a blond, big boned, blue eyes and bout half Sonny's height. That saying "Hell hath no furry like a woman scorned." that saying was made for her. She smoked pot but all other was a sin.

The reply reluctant "All right just long as Deryl ain't home." To Deryl who smoked meth, everything else' was a sin. "And I don't want any of that shit man." That was a lie.

"Good more for me, ha, ha ha ha, I know ya' done quit, I don't want to be a bad influence, but….."

"It's o.k. I can handle the pressure." That was a lie.

With out getting into detail, crack can be smoked off a can. Shep standing in his bedroom with Sonny, a single bed, bedside table and drawer with no lamp, a window to the front yard seeing pecan trees and one to the driveway and the house on the other side the driveway, and against the wall a mirror and chest of drawers.

About the house across the driveway. I didn't give the total lay out of the land before because I didn't want to loose site of what was important. Now, I get to emphasize that it was Russia, and the recipe, in short. Since this chapter is ramblings on of the goings on, the driveway fed two houses. The green cement block house and a cream-colored lapboard with one foot wide boards, no screened in, but a small front porch with steps leading to the front door. Three different bedroom windows to the block house side and three matching den and kitchen windows on the other side. Then a kitchen door opened to the back yard and den door opened to the front porch and front yard with a couple of tall pines. Just Google earth it.

In the cream-colored lap board house resided Shep's cousin, being Deryl's and Andy's older brother Ben, crack addict, hard worker, stubborn, thin good looking, smart, self centered to the point he's hard to get along with for most.

Also living there was Trudy, A pretty girl, a little over weight, keeps her self and surroundings very clean and in order, brown hair medium length always perfectly styled in several different manners.

All right then back to the story, witch is fact, except any part that one is said to be doing something illegal, those parts are fiction. If it were true, they and I could be locked up for breaking the law so those parts are fiction.

I/Shep was standing in the bedroom with Sonny at Deryl's, smoking CRACK! Luckily, Sonny had chumped him off with a taste. A whole hit may have put Shep into full relapse.

Shep quickly opened the bed side drawer and pulled out a piece of tin foil about ten inches long and three inches wide, folded in to a V boat long ways. Reaching in the drawer with the other hand he pulls out a drinking straw and sticks it in his mouth. Striking a lighter holding it under the V of the foil a crystalline substance in the V started to melt and run to the down side the boat, giving off smoke. Shep chased the smoke with the straw inhaling. "Chase the dragon" Shep said holding in the smoke at the same time. He held the foil out to Sonny.

"This that shit you been talking about that's supposed to be so good?" Sonny grabbed the foil and copied Shep. Blowing out a cloud of smoke.

Shep explained, "Don't waste it dude, that's dope your blowing all over the room, hold it in."

Before Sonny put the lighter to the foil again he asked, "Damn, ya' got some this I can take with me."

Reaching under the bed Shep pulled out a roll of aluminum foil and ripped off a peace. "This is all I got right now, it was gave to me. I ain't had to cook a damn thing. I guess it's one of the perks of figuring out the recipe for four counties and God only knows where it's gone now. I'm sure it's collided with other circles that have figured it out too." He broke a little piece of crystallized meth off the foil they were hitting and wrapped it in

Sonny's foil. "Take this to the shed in your back yard cause this shit will funk up the house."

Sonny put the foil in his pocket and headed out the door. "Yea' I should be all right as long as she don't smell it."

Shep laughed, "And avoid eye contact, ya' gonna' be bright eyed."

With a, "Cool man." Sonny was gone.

For the next few weeks Shep and Sonny had this same routine, excluding the Crack part. Shep was enjoying life.

Chapter 5

It was Friday and Shep had got home from work and freshened up, and then went outside. It was a beautiful day. Deryl was still at work or some where. Gabby was touch and go at any day or night or hour. The thing about the meth they were doing, it kept them tinkering and fixing and a lot of taking stuff apart, always going, going, going. Shep picked up a shovel that was leaning against one of the sheds and started shoveling the dirt off the driveway that had built up in spots after years of rain. The grass was taking over the driveway.

A small white hatchback pulled up the driveway, the window rolled down, revealing a blond blue eyed beauty with full lips, high cheek bones, full of life. "Hiya', I'm looking for Deryl."

"He ain't here."

"Well then…" She hesitated as if lost for what to do next.

Shep rescued her. "Ya' wanna' hit some foil?"

The car shut off and the body hooked to that beautiful face got out, the small but firm titts, in a small white T, the tight jeans held a flat tummy, wide hips, and a firm ass with some long legs.

Shep was in instant lust. She looked him in the eye. It was like they had known each other forever. "I'm Barbra" she moved closer.

"I'm Shep, Deryl's cousin."

They moved inside. She hit the foil only like three times and said she'd had enough. They talked about who knew who and where was where. She was Jeffro's exol'lady.

Jeffro was a wiry, goatee sporting cat, liked cowboy boots and cowboy hats. He was also the partner in crime of Gabby that helped Gabby tweak out the details of the recipe. He was in and out the Sanford and Arms quite often and the real reason Barbra had stopped by. The two laughed and talked naturally enjoying each others company.

As she was opening the door to leave she initiated the step in and stole a kiss on the cheek for the road. The door opened and there stood a bug-eyed, smiling, stout fellow with fist in mid knock. "I ain't interrupting am I?"

"Naw" she said "I was just leaving"

"Damn, I was hoping to join in."

Barbra let out a "HA" pushing her way past him, "No means no Al."

Shep noticed she knew his name, and thought she must be the best kept secret in the county. She really didn't seem the easy type, too tough. Maybe that was why; they didn't have the bragging rights.

Al came on in "Hey man I need a hand tonight."

Shep heard the car door shut and turned his attention to Al. "What's up?"

"I'm going on a mission."

"What's in it for me?" Shep said, picking up the foil, and handing it to Al.

He chased the dragon and exhaled a cloud of smoke. Shep started to say something about wastefulness but gave up. Al went to hit the foil again, but managed to give his deal first. "Two eight-balls."

"Doing what?"

"Help me fill some propane tanks with ammonia."

"That anhydrous from Gabby and Deryl ain't good enough for ya'?"

"It cost too much, I want my own."

Shep knew Al could pull off this heist by himself and just needed the company to keep him from chickening out. "Two eight balls? How bought I just get enough ammonia to bring my own cook off, out one of the propane tanks."

The tanks had to have special stainless steal valves on them, and the hose to be hooked up to the tanks had to be versatile. This all took preparations. Time is of importance, not wanting to be caught holding the bag, or tanks in this case.

What Shep would make off this mission would be worth the gamble. At the same time he didn't want to be a big timer on account it seemed to be flirting too much with prison. Truthfully just being where he lived was a pass to prison, he knew it, but it still seemed safer not being a big seller of the product.

That night Al and Shep in a black Z71 pick up truck pulled into a secluded field two counties over. The liquid ammonia is used as fertilizer by farmers with rather large fields. They hooked the make shift hose to the large tank, twice the size of the Z71, and injected the pressurized ammonia from it into 2 valve less propane tanks. After filling the tanks they screwed the stainless steal valves in them and made their getaway.

Two days later Shep had enough pseudophed pills and pulled off his first batch, an ounce of meth. It cost him $125.00 and returned a little over a thousand bucks, with plenty left over to support his habit for a while.

Chapter 6

The sleepless days, nights, and months rolled on. Some where in there Shep lost his job. The tension between him and Deryl grew. New years came, the turn of a century. Shep had been home from the mountains for a little over a year. At the party of Sanford arms, he met a few new folks. Two being a strange duo, being not a couple, but partners in cooking.

The thick rimmed glasses and premature gray hair on the 30 year old medium build man we called All Night was the first noticeable thing about him. His calm and laid back, not to mention his kindness was the second thing.

His partner, Red, 28 short and built like a young girl, most obvious trait is her waist length beautiful dark red hair. Then her drive, off the chain, but aw' inspiring, not get on your nerves off the chain.

Barbra and Gabby were there and even Reba stopped in for a moment. There was Shaky, but Deseray had done run off. Also there, Al, Jeffro, and a good 30 more, it was fun.

January, February, creaped on by, Shep hated the cold weather. He had gone a year and four months with out smoking any crack, except for that chump off from Sonny. A year and five months ago, he thought he would die smoking crack and hated his life.

Shep had spent more time around his son in that year than he had since his son's first few year's of life. Marcus, 9 was at the age of video games and always had friends his age over. Shep tried to talk to him but it was as if it was almost too late. So Shep found himself kicking it with Mathew, Marcus's youngest brother. Shep got along great with the very small for a three-year-old blue eyed curly blond hair, crumb snatcher. He would often baby sit while Tiffany and Shane went out on the town. Zackery the middle son of Shane looked like his daddy spit him out, tall, lanky. Zackery gave Shep a hard time, but Shep did not care he just would just kill him with kindness and it pissed Zack off. Some weeks Shep would keep

Mathew at their house spending day and the night while they were at work and the two older boys at school.

Tiffany was Shep's girlfriend long before he married her. They had met at the skating rink when they were 12 years old and they broke up at 14.

He saw her at a red light intersection when 17. Remembering her phone number all those years. Two years later, they got married. A year later, they got divorced with a 9-month-old son.

The biggest mistake Shep made was not being the man Tiffany needed. Instead; he was a wild catter, a real go-getter, an SOB right down to the letter. Staying out drinking and smoking pot, which they used to do together. Then the cheating started and Shep got caught red handed. She would never be his lover again but she never gave up on him as a friend, not that she always got along with him though.

Tiffany had a job at Geico Insurance, but after the divorce, she accepted a job at the Jones County court house as a judge's secretary. She remarried soon after to Shane. He had a job at a local factory and made a decent check.

Jump forward a year and a half after Shep left for rehab in the mountains. Shep walked up Tiffany and Shane's front steps. The house was rectangle in shape nothing fancy, off white vinyl siding, green shutters, front porch steps reached a porch about five foot off the ground. He opened the glass storm door and knocked on the front door. Tiffany's voice invited him in. She disappeared behind the wall that separated the den from the kitchen that left the dining area in plain view. The couch and love seat looked upon a stone fireplace and entertainment center under a cathedral ceiling.

He dropped his bag of clothes on the floor as little Mathew came running from the kids bedrooms. Shep dropped to one knee and caught him. "Hey lil' buddy, did ya' miss me?"

Mathew jumped from his arms "Play out side" is all he said as he turned and went running back into the bedroom.

"I reckon so" Shep stood up.

Tiffany came back into the room. "Guess who came to see me at work today?"

"Elvis"

"No"

"Jim Morrison"

"No"

"Billy Idol"

"No damn it, a FBI and a CIA agent."

Shep sat on the couch only to be put back on his feet as Mathew came through the room in high gear with plastic bat and ball. "Oh, the Sheriff and his deputies coming over to serenade you at the court house wasn't enough, ya' had to go get some feds?"

She laughed and plopped down on the couch and started messing with the remote to get her recorded soaps on. "Fuck you man. No, they were asking about Deryl. Said he put in an application to go to Russia and do maintenance at the U.S. Embassy. He had me down as a reference."

Shep was halfway out the door. The first thing to pop in his mind was, how long they been in town, cause there has been a lot of cooks and a lot of meth rite there at ground zero. This put his "OH SHIT" on high alert. "Dose Deryl know?"

She knew what was up around there, she would get a capsule of meth every once in awhile, but Shep would only half pack it. "Yes I called him as soon as they left?"

"Good lookin' out."

"Don't mention it."

Shep went out the door "Let's play ball!"

Chapter 7

Two nights later the southern rock group 38 Special was playing at the largest club in Macon. A crew of twelve people had gathered at Deryl's for a before the concert party.

Standing by his open bedroom closet, Shep grabbed a twenty ounce Mountain Dew bottle off the top shelf. He turned and looked at a skinny, thin haired, narrow faced, brown eyed character. "Shep, what ya' got there?" Grimsly asked grinning from ear to ear.

"All Night gave me about fifteen filters the other day." Filters are exactly that. Coffee filters that were used to filter the meth out the organic solvent. After the meth is dumped out the filter there is a good bit stuck to the fiber of the filters. "I put them in this bottle and filled it with distilled water. I'm ganna' filter this and evaporate the water and see how much meth is left.

"Damn Shep, smart. What ya' fixing to do now?"

"Fixin' to drank me some."

"That don't sound smart."

"Shep turned the bottle up, taking a swig, only about half an inch of the mixture was gone. He took another swig, bringing the mixture down about a that much more. The bitterness off it made his face pucker. "Shit man that pretty fucking strong shit man." He held the bottle out to Grimsly. "Take ya' a nip of some of that."

Grimsly grabbed it and took a taste, but just a taste. "I believe I'm bout' geeked up as I wanta' be there man." Handing the bottle back to Shep, the top went back on it and it went back on the top shelf of the closet.

30 minutes later Shep was in the yard with his finger down his throat, wondering if he might die. If he could puke enough out his stomach before it was too late, or if it was too late. The world was spinning and sweat was beading up from head to toe. His shirt, chest and back was soaked in sweat, he took it off. It was cold but the sweat kept coming. Going over to the water spicket, by the shed, he splashed water on his face and head. A girl's voice

snuck up on him. "Ya' could freeze to death boy." Red was standing behind him. All dolled up for the concert. God, she is so pretty.

"Shit girl, I thank I did too much. I'm geeked past the point of geeked."

"I'd say, Grimsly told me what you did, ya' oughta' be more careful. Now get your ass in here and get some milk, that should take the edge off."

"Think it'll work?"

" I don't know but I ain't fixing to leave ya' out here to die."

The first person Shep noticed standing close to the door of the club was Special Agent DEA, Sterling, keeping the peace. By then it was too late, they had made eye to eye contact. "Shep you all right?" Sterling had one eye brow raised.

"Yea, I think every things OK." Shep headed for the up stairs, where the pool table crowd was hanging out. He felt like he was in a strobe light. Every thing was super crisp, and moving fast around him. Bitter-sweet paranoia mixed with shhhhwooooo.

Grabbing a stool at the bar, Shep stood back up to change bar's but it was to late the dude bartender had saw him. The wavy shoulder length hair on the roman looking, well fit, man was Shep's and Deryl's first cousin. He coached college basketball by day and bartended by night. "Shep you all right?"

"Uh, Yea, I need a Budweiser."

"I'd say, it looks like you need a tranquilizer."

Shep smiled and squinted his eye's, "How bout this?"

Robby just shook his head, "Get off that shit man."

Shep looked down at the bar feeling a slight guilt coming on, and nodded his head, turning back into the crowd. The full effects of his tripping kicked back in and the guilt magically disappeared.

Trying to not walk like he felt, Shep made his way back to his group to find Tiffany and Shane saying their hello's. Tiffany looked at Shep "Damn it" She came face to face for an unneeded closer study. "What the hell you doing?"

Shep grinned "Can't say, but I did a lot of it."

She laughed and he noticed she was flicking her finger nails and shifting from foot to foot. He thought of how well he knew her. Knowing she was fixing to surprise him with some news. But, the news was almost no surprise. He had already let it cross his mind on the trip to the concert.

The Music was loud and she got closer to his ear. "Guess who's here."

"Elvis?"

"No"

"Pearl Jam?"

"No"

"The porn star Jessie Jane?"

She punched him in the ribs "No the CIA and FBI agents that came from Washington DC."

"It had crossed my mind."

"You want me to show you them?"

Shep looked around remembering to squint his eyes, only making it look like he was geeked up squinting his eyes. "Hell yea."

She scanned the crowd "If I see them again I'll show you." Her eyes stopped at Shane, who was talking to Gabby, They had went to school together. Her pretty little ass followed her eyes.

Shep tried to look cool strolling around checking out the chicks. He was way too fucked up to make a conversation with any stranger and his shirt was getting sweaty again. The concert was over before Shep knew it and he was ready for it to be. If he had seen the FBI and CIA he didn't know he did. If they had been investigating Deryl, to the point of surveillance they recognized him and the rest of the folks he came with.

Chapter 8

Getting dropped off at home after the concert, Shep was so cranked up he went to his bed room and laid it down, anything else would feel like over load. The quiet house, and being alone started the paranoia. He got up and went to the kitchen, getting a roll of electrical tape from the drawer under the microwave.

Deryl and some girl he had never seen before came in from the outside, just getting home from the concert. Shep ignored them and Deryl returned the favor.

Shep stopped in the bathroom and snuck a compact mirror and the tape by the two trying to score off each other as they settled into the side by side recliners in the living room. They paid him no mind no way.

Back in the dark bedroom he pulled the rod that opens the slats of the blinds off and taped the mirror to the end of it. Laying back in the bed face up he used the mirror as a periscope to peak out the blinds.

The phone rang then Deryl's voice "lil' late for a service call ain't it?...........Shit."

The girls voice "What?"

"Nothing to be concerned about."

Shep's attention was swallowed up by the darkness of the outside reflected through the mirror between the slots he had opened in the slats. He could make out the driveway. Deryl's white work van glowed and the house across the driveway was a gray back drop.

After a while he started seeing what looked like shadow men { dark images} moving around the driveway. They became more and more real as the endless seconds ticked-stopped by. The conversation murmured on in the living room, he couldn't understand it nor was he trying.

He peaked out the blinds with his own eyes only to lay back down insisting to himself he was just tripping. It wasn't long, the mirror was raised up and he clearly saw two shadow men up by the other house. Getting out of the bed, for the fact that he knew he had saw what he saw, and knocking to get out his own bed room door was debatable, he did it anyway. The two were still sitting next to each other with a boat of foil laying between them. The strong smell of fresh cut grass with a pungent twist was very noticeable. The meth smelt like that.

Deryl's introduction "This is my fucked up cousin, that needs to go back to bed. He's been up for 14 days."

"Man I saw some folks in the driveway sneaking around."

The girl busted into a laugh "DAMN IT boy"

Deryl rolled his eye's " See what I mean? Go back to bed Taiter head"

Shep knew how crazy he was looking "Good idea. Don't do nothing I wouldn't do."

The mirror went back to it's view point, Shep laid there with nothing better to do, peeking peaked. It was all fun and games till the two shadow's made their encore in cam frog suits and nuclear holocaust gas mask. One of them came right to the window investigating.

Shep whispered with a hint of voice to try and let the outsiders know that they had been made. At the same time he tried to not to be heard by his cousin and company. " Fucking frog suits and nuclear mask. I see it."

The next day and on past the next night Shep was in a deep state of sleep. Around Noon, that day, he woke up to a new stranger. She was standing over him, just looking. Dark blond hair loosely pulled to a puffy pony tail, round blue eyes, short, with a round ass and round tit's. "Hey" she said.

"I can't believe I fell asleep, I guess I flipped the script."

"You been out for a day and a half."

"I needed it. What's your name? Blue Eyes?"

"She smiled, "No it's Amy."

"Are you an angel?"

"No, Grimsly went to Wal-Mart with your cousin and told me to keep an eye on you."

"Watch me sleep?"

"No they said if you wake up to take that Base Ball bat in there and knock you back out."

Red came busting in the room "I thought you done came awake. Get your ass up don't sleep your life away."

Shep stood up out the bed, opposite side Amy, not wanting to come on to strong with the half swollen tent his boxers were sporting.

Red grabbed Amy by the arm and fled to the living room were Kid Rock could be heard at a mellow volume. " Get ya' britches on. We'll be in here."

Two days later Shep was packing his stuff in a card board box and carrying it across the driveway to live with Trudy and Ben.

Chapter 9

This book has been autobiographical to Shep's perspective and will remain so. I/Shep could only imagine and speculate what happened when I was not around. I'm just showing how things could have realistically happened. I was checking things out from many angles. I never put all faith in the things I didn't have out-rite proof , but I did have reason to think it possible and rhyme to bring it to view. This is from DEA agent and product of Gailu dr., Sterling's perspective {and my just maybe's} after the concert.

The crowd was gone, Sterling took a seat at Robby's bar. "Long time no see." They had grown up across the street from each other on Gailu dr. and both 6+ years Shep and Deryl.

Robby opened the cooler "You want a beer?"

"I suppose they owe me that much."

They both nursed on a beer and caught up on old times and new ones. A man in a suit with no tie walked by and put 500 dollars on the bar in front of Sterling and kept walking. Sterling picked it up then threw the beer bottle in the trash from half way cross the bar. He winked at Robby "One for you coach." He picked the cash up, "Not bad, four hours of work and only one half ass fight."

Robby wiped the arm of his short sleeve shirt over his forehead still cooling down from the nonstop serving. "Did ya' see my cousin's?"

"Yea, I talked to Deryl, I don't think he'll be going to the embassy in Russia."

Robby lacked astonishment "Did I miss something?"

"Deryl had his paper work in to do maintenance work at the U.S. Embassy. Washington sent a FBI agent and CIA agent to check him out. They been here for a few days, they was here tonight. They came to see me I was a reference."

Robby started wiping the bar down. Sterling kept on with his story, "They said your cousins are flirting with disaster. Which I already knew, I had my eyes and ears on them, unofficially , for a while now. I'm glad Shep ain't smoking crack so, but well ……..and damn they having a good time."

Robby leaned his elbows on the bar and looked Sterling in the eye. He knew cooking meth was big trouble. "You going to give them fair warning?"

"Hell yea, fair warning." He pulled out his phone and scrolled through to A/C repair man, hitting the send. "Deryl this is Sterling,"

Deryl looked at the girl sitting beside him in the matching recliners, the foil of meth laying between them. His eyes widened wider. "Little late for a service call ain't it?"

`Sterling started for the exit "If y'all don't stop doing ya' going down like dick suckin' clowns." Killing the phone, "Take care Robby."

"You too man."

Sterling got in his green F-150 truck, with blue stripe on the front tag. Pulling out the club he flicked the switch on a box under the dash and smiled. From a speaker in the box under the dash came the sound of breathing and shuffling, a knock, "This is my fucked up cousin that needs to go back to bed, he's been up for like 14 days."

"Man I saw some folks in the driveway sneaking around."

A girl's voice busted into a laugh "DAMNIT boy."

Deryl's voice " See what I mean? Go back to bed Taiter head"

"Yea good idea. y'all don't do nothing I wouldn't do."

Sterling heard the door shut and more scuffling. He stopped at a gas station. After fueling up he started on his way home listening to more scuffling around then silence. " Fucking frog suits and nuclear mask. I see it." More silence, a few miles later he heard semi familiar voices, but quickly silenced.

Sterling turned the truck toward Dry Branch. He was afraid of what to expect. He parked at Hortman's Grocery Store on Hwy. 80 about 100 yards before Deryl's. Hiking down the hill of 80, he cut up in the woods coming out at the house beside Deryl's he stood behind the corner, scoping out the situation.

From the back door of Deryl's he witnessed the frog suits emerging from within. A weird site to see in Dry Branch, GA. When they got in the driveway between the houses the mask and hoods came off the suits. The CIA and FBI agents looked around.

Sterling came into the open. "What the hell's going on around here?"

The two agents didn't even seem startled. It was like they expected Sterling to be there. The CIA agent responded. "We put the house to sleep with sleeping fog and made Shep swallow some nanobugs."

Sterling standing with his arms crossed over his chest. "Nano what?"

The FBI agent spoke up "He's our human bug now Sterling."

Sterling did his best James Dean " What the fuck dose that mean, is it going to fuck him up, he's a friend of mine."

The frog suits were being striped off in a rush, no telling what hour somebody could pull in the driveway. The FBI agent shook his head. "We don't know the long term effects of it. He's not the first, but not far from it. As far as we know."

They decided to continue the conversation at a better place and time. They listened for a day and a half of Shep talking in his sleep and gibberish of the company in the other rooms that sounded as that, voices from another room. The FBI and CIA from their new human bug and Sterling from his house bug.

Chapter 10

Two days later the three agents planned to meet up at the DEA office in an office building on the out skirts of Macon. Sterling arrived first. Entering an office with a small four chair waiting area, a very artistic copper sailing ship hung on the wall in 3-D, a door opposite the entrance, and glass partition with a shelf under it with a receptionist desk behind that.

No one was in view so he felt under the comer of the shelf and pressed a hidden button, The door opposite the entrance clicked. Opening to a small interviewing room, small table three chairs and a filing cabinet. The other door in that room led into a cement block hallway, no paint, concrete floor, bare.

Halfway down the hallway he sat in his office, flicking on a house bug box he tuned it to Deryl's. A buzzer alerted him to see, on his computer, the two human bug makers enter the waiting room.

The three of them gathered in a back office, the sunlight brightened the room from a full wall window that over looked 1-75 speeding by from Atlanta to Florida and back to Atlanta.

Sterling had his bug box and plugged it in. It started making a hissing noise with REO Speed Wagon playing softly in the background. "They done took it down a few levels since I gave a warning and I noticed Shep ain't spontaneously combusted yet from them nano's."

The CIA agent pulled a small flip phone from his pocket. "This is the upgrade of the bug. This transceiver is yours. Open it up and power it up like any cell phone, enter B-U-G-l and the bottom right key.

It just so happened the phone and Sterling's box came alive with Reds voice. "Boy, get out that window, quit staring, what ya' see out there?"

Shep was staring past the pecan trees, across hwy. 80, and halfway across a plowed field. "See that stump over there in that field?"

Red turned up the stereo a little "It looks like the same stump that was there since that tree hit the ground."

Shep agreed "It damn dose don't it and I been looking at it like somebody's behind it looking at our empty yard."

Red changed the subject "Better get to packing if ya'; cuzz pulls up and you ain't moved out, the shit gonna' hit the fan."

"I'm done, all I got is a box of clothes and a few nick-knacks. I'm gonna miss you Red." He reached out for a good by hug.

She flung her long red hair around as she left him standing crazy. "You just going across the driveway."

Sterling interrupted the ease dropping "So now what?"

The FBI agent said. "Hell, we don't know yet, this is our first human bug too."

The CIA agent laughed and shook his head "I got an idea and it doesn't include locking him up."

Sterling agreed with that so far. "That would be dirty to do what ever the fuck y'all did to him and then lock him up, besides what good is it if he's locked up." He had a quick after thought and blurted it out. "The meth's sure took a lot of the traffic out the crack traps. It ain't no better but it is I guess."

The agents turned their attention back to the sound's coming from the bug Sterling had planted in the house and the sound over the bug

phone that was from the bugs in Shep. The box was playing Red singing out of key to the stereo. The phone was playing Shep's voice across the driveway
letting his new live in land-lord, Trudy know she didn't have to worry, that he'd behave.

Sterling rolled his eyes at Shep's lie. "Anyway the politicians up there in your neck of the woods are dragging their feet. They should have took the cold pills off the shelf by now. That's the only thing that's going to slow it down."

The other two agent's both agreed and let Sterling know they had a surprise for him later that night. They were waiting for an app to be sent to the phones.

Later in the evening the agents sat by the pool surrounded by a rod iron fence, under the security lights of the Howard Johnson Inn. The traffic of the busy Riverside Drive steadily zoomed by. Blair the FBI agent had his phone out, looking at a lit screen of files and such.

Martin the CIA agent spoke in a quiet voice. "How long you been listening to Shep, or the house bug, I should say?"

Sterling relaxed in his chair. "I snuck in and planted the bugs a month ago or so."

Martin smiled. "We noticed what was going on right off the rip when we got to town and started investigating, We reported to head quarters what we had discovered and a few hours later we unexpectedly got a call informing us we were in charge, so to speak, of "The Nannobugged

Experiment" to pick a lab rat, a person engaged in meth lab activity, and bug him. We picked Shep due to the way he stood out at the 38 special concert and of course we had seen him at Deryl's."

Sterling gave his approval " Well, I have learned from the house bug that he was the one that sparked the fire for this area a year and a half ago. Crazy son of a bitch looked it up in chemistry books and encyclopedias, I heard Grimsly telling somebody all about it just the other day."

The phone Blair was fiddling with chimed. They could hear Shep's voice in mid-sentence. " ..... where I'd stay if it wasn't for you and Ben. Darby can still pick me up, we got a lot of houses to fix up so he can rent them out. " Then Trudy's voice laughing, "You so crazy, I don't mind you living here, just pay your share of the bills and don't have traffic in and out."
"Thanks, well Darby will be here early in the morning to pick me up so I'm gonna' lay it down."

The three agents listening to the bug phone heard a door shut, some shuffling around and the low talk of the TV Trudy was watching, soon paralleled Shep's steady breathing as he laid in his bed thinking about life.
Blair got up and started moving toward the iron gate of the pool fence. "Come on." He led Martin and Sterling to his room in the breezeway near the pool. They entered his room, standing by the window that out looked to the breezeway he reached down to cut the air conditioner off and gave the "shhh" sign with a finger to his lips. He hit a code of keys on the phone and laid it on the air conditioner unit just under the window. Motioning the CIA and DEA agents back out into the breezeway he shut the door extra softly.

Standing at the window Blair started talking at the window as if to some one in the motel room. This is what Shep heard as he laid in his bed back in Dry Branch, his mind, his ears, his common senses putting the voice out side his window. "Shep you think you can start this wildfire and just step away?" It sounded exactly real.

Martin noticed a Funnel Web Spider peeking out a crack between the window and the wall, coupling it with a baseball bat bag he had seen a motel guest with, in the parking lot earlier. "Yea Shep, your caught up in the web now and we're the Brown Recluses. Soon as you go to sleep we're going to sodomize you with this base ball bat."

Blair and Sterling looked at Martin with every facial expression of "God Damn!"

Sterling wasn't sure if what he thought was going on was really happening or not. He was wondering if this was a joke and the folks from the DEA office would come laughing around the corner any second.

Shep sat up in his bed "While y'all bullshithin'."

The agents listened to Shep's voice coming from the phone, from in side the motel room. Sterling put his two cents in. "Yea, mother fucker, one two we coming for you, three, four better lock your door."

Blair was opening the door to the room giving them the "shhhh" sign again. Once in side he pushed one key on the phone. "OK now we can hear him but he can't hear us."

Sterling was smiling from ear to ear in disbelief. "What have I got my self into?"

Martin tried to explain, while the sound of Shep going out the back door of the house into the darkness in Dry Branch came over the phone. "It's like he's got MRI juice in him." He paused to hear Shep foolishly look for evidence of the Brown Recluses "I can't see shit out here, and ain't sure if I want to." Martin continued "Anyway, Like a MRI except all we need is a satellite that picks up the nano-hertz band width and instead of images we get sound and send sound, At least that's my guess it's top secret stuff, that out ranks me."

Sterling was starring at him still tripping on what just happened "Ya', don't say?"

Blair represented the FBI "I don't know, I cant say."

Shep could be heard going back into his room. He knew better than to mention any thing to Trudy on account he didn't have any where but there to live.

The sound of a line of meth was heard being chopped up on a plate. The agents expected it must be a gangster of a line from all the chopping. They didn't know the half of it. After a long hard snort "Fuckin' a that'll blow the back of your head off, damn it boy." As he rubbed his hand to the right side of his face pressing for some relief.

Blair turned the bug phone off. "Me and Martin got to be on a jet in the morning headed to the mountains. I'll show you how to operate your bug phone. May be best if you come up with an idea that follows our story line, to keep things interesting. you know what I mean?"

Sterling felt a bit nervous as the surprise wore thin. "I dig what ya' saying."

Chapter 11

Blair and Martin were posted up in the back of a military jeep going up a mountain road. They cleared a check point then another, then sat two massive thick reinforced doors that opened to a tunnel, the jeep disappeared into the side of the mountain.

A tile floor room consisting of a desk with a laptop on it where sat a Brad Pitt looking scientist, a couch where sat Blair and Martin, in front of a large flat TV, and a few swimsuit model posters hung on the wall.

(This is where the story turns greatly to a mental perception as apposed to a conspiracy theory, due to the technology. I/Shep keep it true to my perception at the time and did not let it discourage the over all mission of this book. Our minds in general can be persuaded to believe in so many things and in some cases to do what seems as outrages acts to many, seems most logical to the beholder. Example: The many religions of the world. Some even dance with rattle snakes.)

The scientist at the computer hit a final hard tap on the key board. Walking over to the TV he pointed at the display as he explained. " Check this out." The screen flickered and a thin blue line appeared across it. "I have some examples of how this works. The line represents and is the brain waves of a rat finding it's way through a maze. Notice the distortion of the line, much like a heart monitor going crazy. Now using a computer to find some method in the madness of thought pattern, I have some examples of this also." The screen flicked off and back on with the blue line across it. "The first time the rat goes through the maze, that is now, notice the number of distortions. Now this is the fifth time, with fewer distortions. This rat already knows the maze so it takes about the same amount of time to run through the maze. This is the 15th time, notice two distinct patterns. That's because the computer has done its work by matching up the rats brain waves with sensors in the maze sensing weather the rat takes a left or right."

Martin spoke up. "So the computer knows the brain wave of this rat for left and right."

The scientist sat in his chair at the desk, back straight, eyes wide open, and dramatically reaching out with his arms "GOD IS DEAD!" He got blank looks from the two agents, so he decided to explain. I've always wanted to say that, I've been working on my delivery. What you think?" The two agents gave a slow applause.

The scientist gave a few nods of gratitude then went to explaining. "Since the nanobugs are attached throughout the nervous system and they send out the electrical signals from the shift of ions that is the electrical current of living things, and being that the brain waves of speech are among the strongest because it fires so many neurons at such distinct levels and patterns they are easy to map, „per say. So with nanobugs in a human, the computer can map out the speech and the surrounding sounds linking it to thought patterns. Of course as with the rat each person is unique."

The agents, although a bit bewildered by the sensitivity and accuracy of the technology, followed what the man was preaching. Martin asked about the brain wave signals via nanobugs being strong enough to be received in space. He was reminded that there are GPS trackers implanted in humans and animals the size of a grain of rice and how the collection of neurons firing to produce the words we are thinking are as a group much larger than a grain of rice.

They discussed Shep and brainstormed plans of how to go about doing what the hell ever they were going to do. They laid some basics down but decided that due to the unknown variables that may arise they would just wing it for the most part and build on what the Brown Recluses had started. They still had a little while till Shep's thought pattern was completely mapped.

Chapter 12

Sterling was sitting at his desk at the DEA office, the buzzer alerted him of company. The computer screen showed Blair an Martin in the waiting area. He greeted them and led them to his office.

Sterling said "I've been thinking while y'all were gone. How bout' we just talk to him at night."

Martin, as if to butt in, laid his bug phone on the desk as an example. "Get a load of this, we didn't explain this by the pool the other night. These bug phones have four microphones in them giving the illusion of depth to our sound in Shep's ears. Since the crystals in the nanobugs are vibrating in the same nerves his ear drum ends up vibrating on, his mind and our acoustics put it from where he thinks the sound is coming from."

Blair added with a grin of uncontrollable excitement, "And that ain't shit wait till you see what's next."

Martin cut him off, "But that's at a later date"

Blair relaxed a tad bit. "Yea later, but you wait and see."

They discussed their plans for that evening. They had to be ready to make a good impression on their human bug.

That night Shep was alone in the house. Ben, Deryl's oldest brother, Shep's cuz- housemate, was God only knows where. Trudy was spending the night at her mom's to go to the doctor early the next morning. Trudy has only one kidney and did that often.

Shep was in his room popping phsudophed pills out of blister packs for a cook of meth later that week. From the window he heard "Shep, Shep, this is the Brown Recluses, We noticed you been staying up all night."

Shep put the blister pack down and crept over to the window. Grabbing the string on the blinds with a quick jerk, snatching down on the string. Instead of the blinds going up, they came out of their brackets and with a crash hit the blackness of the window, the window seal and the floor. The light in the room produced a glare on the window and Shep could not see out very well, but he could hear the sound of feet running and voices "go, go, go" and some laughing.

Shep was prepared due to the last threats of sodomization. He took up an Ax handle that was leaning in the corner by his bedroom door. Going through the den headed for the front door thinking "This is crazy, it's got to be my head going crazy, really who's going to really take time to fuck with me at my window, but it sounded so real, so loud and clear, not like shadow voices, but maybe Sterling would pull some cracker jack shit like this, scare tactics."   .

By this time Shep was creeping around the yard with an ax handle propped on his shoulder looking around all corners of the house. Across the driveway sat Deryl's white van and a dark empty house. Realizing how crazy he must look he decided to go back in the house before someone turned in the driveway and lit him up with their headlights.

He hung the blinds back up and added a few extra screws to stabilize them. Getting out a LED camping light lantern, he gave a soft glow to the room after he turned the over head light out. He finished popping the pills from the blister packs, got a coffee bean grinder from his chestier drawer and grinded the pills to a powder. Standing in front of the kitchen window he put the powder in a zip lock bag. The voices redeemed them selves from outside the kitchen window. "Hey Shep, you can't run us off that easy."

Then another voice, "Hey Shep, Sterling's making me do this .... damn it don't hit me, he frogged me Shep."

"Well you ain't sposed to tell him that
Sonny."
A laugh, "I couldn't help it."

Shep noticed it did sound like Sonny's voice but it also could have been Sterling's. What if Sterling was making his brother do this because he was getting meth from Shep and this was the pay back. Standing there holding the powdered up pills by the kitchen window he, he started to smile. Weather this was all his brain gone haywire or somebody really outside the window, in the darkness of the night, it was some crazy exciting shit.

The back door being in the kitchen he went out to have a look around. All he heard was the sound of a whippoorwill singing it's lonesome song in the woods beside the field behind the back yard. Suddenly that's how he felt to, alone.

Back inside from his lightless room he peeked out the blinds at Deryl's then pulled the blinds up . Taking the zip lock bag out his pocket he hid it in a drawer. He left the blinds up and lights out listening. After a little while he opened the window just a little bit to hear better. The sound of the whippoorwill is all he heard.

On their way to work the next morning Darby was telling Shep all about something, but Shep's mind was on the voices at the window, how clear and plain he could hear them. They sounded so real. Of course he didn't share this with Darby for sake of sounding crazy as a loon.

They were real for all Shep could tell, except for the insane idea that there would be some folks at his window called the Brown Recluses talking about sodomizing him with a baseball bat, and Sonny in on it too, and Sterling going to that length to scare him. Would he? He felt that something was up, more than imaginary voices. Although he knew the mind was a powerful thing and could trick itself into believing things with a lot less persuasion than his had been subjected to.

Chapter 13

After a week with a paranoid ear to the window, with nothing to hear, Shep found himself alone again as for his housemates. This night he was in the kitchen getting a glass of tea. They started at the kitchen window "Shep it's the Brown Recluses, weeeer baaaack."

This time they had multiplied, a new voice was heard, sounding like somebody over acting in a forceful way "Yea Shep we've got the house surrounded tonight, we're coming in."

Shep got a little nervous, so he went to his room and locked the door. He took out his lantern, opened the window a little, as to hear better, but leaving the blinds down. He peeked out at Deryl's house, dark and quiet the van was gone.

Shep felt he needed a boost of fight and he found it in the comer of a baggy and laid a line of adrenaline out on his dresser. With a long snort and a "GOD DAMN THAT BURNS" he pressed his palms to his cheek bones pressing for relief. To himself and loud enough to be heard by his, maybe imaginary foes in the nights yard, he wagered "Hell I'm wired to the max, I'll kill as many of y'all as I can tonight, bring it on."

A new voice came from outside, sounding as if it may be under or down toward the corner of the house. "Shep you ain't killing anybody."

Then the voice of Sterling, "Nobody but yourself."

Sterling, Blair and Martin had taken on two more agents from the DEA office. A straight out skinny nark looking dude, twenty eight years old, in tight jeans and a Hard Rock Café t-shirt, long shoulder length frizzy black hair. He worked on the surveillance equipment and as a confidential informant, giving him a alligator mouth and a humming bird ass.

The other new agent was laid back, prep hair cut, pull over polo shirt, and Dockers pants 30 something in age.

The five agents sat in a room at the Howard Johnson Inn, 1 double bed, a kitchenette, a small round table surrounded by chairs, chestier drawers, T. V. and a couch. They all had a faster pulse from Shep talking about killing them.

The Bug phone was on the table with a shoe box over it, giving Shep the illusion of voices outside the house. (For the sake of names, I/ Shep, called the nark Dumbass.) Dumbass leaned to the box real close to speak but was quickly snatched back by Sterling who said "Not to close to the window, he'll see you." then he winked at Dumbass who gave a thumbs up in return. The nark sat on the bed where his voice would sound further off, it worked. Shep heard a voice over by Deryl's house. "Yea Shep, your only hurting yourself, those that love you and other innocent people with that meth."

Martin removed the box from over the phone shutting it down quickly. "OK we need to talk about some things. I was going to save this for later, but we may as well put it to good use now. He went in his suitcase and pulled out a computer tablet. After a few minutes of the Brown Recluses, not asking, but patiently waiting to see what Martin had in store. The new agents received their own bug phones, he instructed them on powering them up.

Blair knowing what was up, rolled a drum roll with his fingers on the table "Y'all don't go getting a God complex now" looking Dumbass, Prep, and Sterling each in the eyes an grinning.

The three DEA agents turned their attentions to Martin with blank looks, no where near expecting what they were about to witness. Martin passed out some Bluetooth ear buds then tapped on the tablet screen. "Power up the ear buds, so your phones will synch with your ear buds. I can't stress enough for total silence during this presentation." With some codes and programming they all heard the same thing on their ear buds. A realistic computer voice but noticeably a computer talking fast, skipping and gargling some words, with a hiss in the background.

The computer voice in the Bluetooth, ear buds in mid talk opened with, " ..... ut who and how, speakers maybe, under the house, I'm staying in the house tonight, how could they do this, if my brain ain't haywire/fubar, fucked up beyond all repair, they can't really be out there, sounds just like it......"

The Brown Recluses heard from the speaker of the bug phone on the table something different. They didn't hear any talking just Shep moving about the house, doors opening and shutting the water faucet running in a sink. But on the ear buds the fast computer talk kept babbling on "...onna think if it gets out I'm hearing people at the window, there going to think, where my toothbrush, toothpaste, here it is damn HOT, 27,28 how old am I, still cut on wrong one, cause I got toothbrush in right hand, I got to get a girl friend while I still got teeth, Barbra, Tiffany I'd like to see that girl Christy again from the new years party, and way back ninety-two, THE FINAL CHAPTER I miss that bar, met Reba there and Christy, Tammy.(The sound of the tooth brush scrubbing at his teeth played out on the bug phone on the table) Christy, green eyes so sexy, small girl, (Shep's mind pictured a beach with him and Christy on it but just the picture in his mind a split second) Savanna what happened to that Tabatha girl (the computer voice carried on) useta' go Stone Creek Baptist, me and her and that red head stranded on riverfront street they had that softball tournament me and Randy left the FINAL CHAPTER to go meet his girl Wimberley down there they left us stranded 2am, six preps in motorboat want go for a ride, Tabatha had to be drunk or just a freak, both, You ain't my daddy, You ain't going, I tried to stop her. that red head I have no idea what her name was snapped at me, fuck her, let her go. She wasn't gone too long but long enough, she was OK, guess she was smiling, got what she wanted, (By this time the bug phone on the table was playing Shep moving about opening and shutting drawers.) Where is that Cheri magazine, (The ear bud was saying) under here......"

Sterling ran his finger across his throat to Martin who, shut the phone off on the table, there by killing the ear buds also.

Sterling said "Holy Shit bug man."

The prep agent, Prep said with hesitation and eyes shifting back and forth at Martin and Blair" I don't believe this, y'all are trying to trick me."

Dumbass stood from his seat on the bed. "Where's the candid cameras, jokes over, nobody's reading minds, even if you was y'all wouldn't expose it to me and preppy here."

Sterling assured him, "It is a surprise to me too. Believe me if I had known about it, there's no damn way I would have brought you in on it. I don't think I would have brought ME in on it."

Prep accepted the mission, " Count me in, my lips are sealed."

Blair assured them, "Men it is true, so go ahead and let it sink in, I know it is kind of mind boggling at first. Also let me add, in order for us to continue with our charades we must be very careful not to comment on what the ear buds are saying. If he notices us reading his mind, he'll totally rule out us being at his window."

As they sat in silence the blue flash of heat lightning around and in the part of the curtains was noticed by Prep. "How far away is he from here?"

Sterling answered, "Dry Branch, oh, that's about ten miles away as the crow fly's."

Prep nodded his head slightly and rubbed the palm of his hands together in deep thought. "Check this out. ..... " He laid out his plan.

Blair powered up his bug phone. Very quietly he wrapped a towel around it and placed it on the towel wrack near the fart fan in the bathroom and turned it on.

Sterling put his phone in the kitchen cabinet to produce the effect of being some were across the yard. He said, so Shep could hear him, just as he saw the heat lightning light up the black sky of the night with no thunder. It was perfect. "Shep we got company, it looks like a spaceship."

Shep was already at the window just noticing the heat lightning flashing lightly across the sky. His window facing opposite of Macon so the light was coming from behind him. The voices sounded as if they were out of site, with their sound muffling through the walls of the house and there was a humming that seemed to be coming from no where. The ear buds in the agents ears gave them his thoughts on the unbelievable situation. "Alien ships?"

The heat lightning lit up the Howard Johnson paring lot with a day light appearances of consecutive flashes. This bright display carried over to Shep's window with a fairly good glow in the sky. Sterling jumped on it and his voice rode it to Shep's yard. "Oh my god I've never seen any thing like it. Shep this is fucking crazy man, its rite there in the sky, holy shit!"

Prep sounding amazed asked Martin. "Is that some area 51 technology?"

The ear buds in the computer voice was constant in babble of Shep's thoughts " .... This is to fucking crazy, I like it, it's too real, crazy, lithium, too much lithium, that's what they say, what do they know anyway .... "

Dumbass spoke up " Is that our technology or alien technology?"

Shep couldn't help saying out loud, to be heard through the pane of glass that separated him from he UFO that was somewhere behind him out of his view, " HELL YEA' I WANT TO SEE ALIENS."

The yard lit up in a few slow bright flashes as Martin happened to be explaining, "Aliens are real but that's man flying that one. The magnetic field caused by the generation of antimatter that causes levitation of the craft is what sets off that light flashing when its that close to the ground."

The ear buds in the agent's ears with Shep's thoughts in the fast computer voice kept the pace. His mind was running back over memories of X files, Mork and Mindy, Dr. Stephen Hawkins, Ziggy Stardust and the Spiders from Mars. "Close to the ground how close?"

Dumbass gave his best drama impression. "I can feel the static electricity from it. Why is it here?"

With nothing better to say Blair answered. "Coincident I guess"

Shep was enjoying the show. Not believing it, but it was so real it was hard not to believe. The hummm of the UFO had him wondering what was really going on. It was as if as if it were coming from every where. The

Blue tooth alerted the Brown Recluses of Shep's next move. "Maybe I need to go out there and see this for myself." He felt like his hair on his arms was standing, probably because of the hint of statistic electricity earlier in the plot. He had to find his shoes and grab the ax handle giving the renegade cops a little time to prepare.

Sterling spontaneously jumped into action with an idea that he was pondering since the spaceship had arrived. Running his finger across his throat and pointing to the bathroom, he sprang over to the *A/C* unit and turned it on low. By that time Blair was in the bathroom carefully unrolling the phone from the towel. Sterling had gotten his phone from in the cabinet taking it to the *A/C* unit he laid it beside it. Blair had cut his phone off in time with the new space ship sound.

Shep was in the den with ax handle and shoes tied, near opening the front door when he heard the spaceship rev up as Sterling clicked the fan on the *A/C* unit up to med. Shep paused with attention and the spaceship got louder as the *A/C* unit was taken to the high setting. Shep had his hand on the door knob opening the door as he listen to the anti-matter of the ship on full charge start to leave the area.

Sterling looking like he was the worlds for-most expert, like he had had a special gift, as he started clicking the unit down tapping his finger in the air to count the perfect timing he possessed for *A/C* units leaving for hyperspace. The other agents in the room feeling like they needed to help in some way nodded their grinning heads to his orchestration.

With the UFO gone Blair realized they still had to deal with Shep making his descent down the front porch steps. He motioned Sterling to put the phone into the drawer at one end of the kitchen counter. Beckoning Martin to come join in, he led by example tapping his index fingers from the phone end of the counter to the opposite end with Sterling and Martin behind him. The phone in the drawer picked up the slap slap slap fading away and broadcasted it to Shep.

Shep stood in the front-yard ax handle ready for aliens {just in case} listening to the sound of the Brown Recluses running up Hwy. 80. The faint voice of Dumbass asked with a controlled holler. "Did somebody grab the UFO sound box?" Prep mimicked the holler "I got it." The lightning lit up the front yard showing Shep and the condition of his aloneness.

The ear buds gave the Recluses a look inside of the mind of a good sport as Shep thought in the computer voice "... They trick me, that was a good one, had me guessing, it's so real, a sound box making that humming noise sound, how they know the heat lightning would be here, Weather Channel I reckon ...." What was smiles started turning to a contagious laugh as the agents heard him think and say out loud, "Well I'll know' em when I see' em cause by the sound of pitter-patter on that pavement they all be wearing cowboy boots."

Shep eazed on back in the house, folded up a piece of foil and chased the dragon into the strange night, thinking, "What if's and could be's." The agents went there separate ways, adrenalin pumping, they chased their on dragons right through the dawn.

Chapter 14

Shep, wearing cut off at the knees jeans and worn out Reebok tennis-shoes, was putting the push mower up in his parents small tin shed in their back yard. They had went to the Tennessee mountains for a week on a marriage retreat. He had decided to help his dad out by cutting the grass.

Frank and Louise had been married for thirty years and it was as right as rain. Frank is a Vietnam vet and Louise has been his one and only since he had met her on his way through Macon, Georgia in rout home to North Carolina after the war. He didn't really have much to go home to so they stayed in Dry Branch, just East of Macon, where her daddy owned Hortman's Grocery.

Frank ended up with a job working on cranes and other heavy equipment in the chalk minds of the surrounding counties. Louise took some schooling on fixing hair styles of the day and opened her on Shop behind her daddy's store, Hortman's Grocery. The same store on Hwy. 80 just up from Deryl's and Gailu dr.. The name Gailu was formed from Shep's aunt Gail's name, Whom was killed in a car wreck in '65' and his mamma's name.

Granddaddy Walter Hortman had inherited the store from his dad Robert Edward Hortman. When Walter became to ill with emphysema to operate the store he turned it over to his brothers Bill and Phillip.

The store was the last sign of what Dry Branch was back in the day. The building is still there and it's still a store but it's not THE STORE. The land had been least all them years and when the lease had ran out the owner decided he would buy out the store and try his hand at it. It was a failing cause, folks where just passing buy going to the big super stores in Macon.

So it was sold, lock, stock and barrel, to the Patel's. They are nice people. That's bout' the time the Georgia Lottery was legalized and the store reaped the benefits' of gambling addiction.

What Shep remembers from his childhood and early teen years was a store that kinda' would have fit in Mayberry. It had a garage that was connected to it. A slim, tall, bald, cap wearing fellow with large ears and nose, and bright blue eyes, answered to the name of Hurly Kelly, pumped the gas and changed oil and other repairs and up keep to automobiles. He could keep a ash on his cigarette from light up to the butt and not miss a lick of what ever he was doing at the moment. He'd say "Morn'n Glory and How bout' cain fisher."

There was the hang abouts' like one of the older teen boys, that happened to live on Gailu dr. Mark Camron looking like 70's pot head long blond hair all in his eyes who invented the "BIP" that lasted for years, never done the same way twice. There happened to be a crowd in the store that day, shopping and chewing the fat, when the Coca-Cola man was unloading his crates of glass bottles off the truck on to a hand dolly. No one was paying it any attention, except for Mark who just happened to be looking out the long store front window. He hollered "Damn it the Coke man just busted his ass and all them cokes just busted on the pavement." He step back as the window began to line up with folks trying to see the coke mans folly. Marked walked behind them slapping each one hard on the top of the head with a "BIP, BIP, BIP, BIP, BIP, BIP BIP, BIP, and the "BIP" was born.

Shep spent a many a day up at the store as a kid, riding his bike up the trail that cut through the woods from the turn a round end of Gailu dr. and came out behind the store. He'd get a Mellow Yellow and peanut M&M's sit on the paper bag box and at the end of the counter by the glass doors and the cash register, listening to the tales of others. He never saying a word. When Hurly Kelly took his week vacation Bill and Phillip would pay Shep to pump gas.

Shep pushed his dad's lawnmower on to the back of the Shed. Grabbing his shirt off a table in the back to wipe the sweat from his face and neck a girls voice behind him made it's presence "Boo" He turned around to see Red standing in a too large of a white t-shirt, her black bikini bathing suit showing through.

She continued "They told me I would find you down here."

Beside the storage shed was a big in ground cement pool that was courtesy of the late granddaddy Walter Hortman. Excavating and pool's was one of his many endeavors.

Shep smiled "Looks like you want to go for a swim."

She replied jokingly "And it looks like you need too."

He fired up a cigarette "Sounds good to me."

After a dip in the pool they laid back on lounge chairs. Red rung her long dark red hair out "So them folks still coming to your window?"

"Hell yea', and I think they came to my work the other day, hid in the attic, or somebody killed somebody up there."

Red sat up and exuberantly looked at him. "What the hell are you talking about? Boy I am going to stop feeding you that powdery white substance. Deryl's right this time, you have done lost your mind. You got to get some sleep."

Shep laughed "While ya' bullshitin', I'm O.K. it ain't the dope or the sleep, Ya know what it might be, it might be nanotechnology, that's technology built on a molecular scale, and I was reading a electronics book the other day and it's easy to build an a.m. radio with two crystals and a piece of copper wire that don't take no battery, just the radio wave is all it needs, so what if they mixed up some copper, crystal and amino acids that will combine with the nervous system and slipped it to me and now its combined with my nerves and now I'm a fucking walking walky-talky. I mean I'm just saying, what if?"

Red was laid back eyes closed taking it all in, "hmm" she grunted, "Well since you put it like that, now I'm not sure. But I still can't help thinking you blew a fuse the night we went to the 38 Special concert."

"Well they was all there at the concert, you know that, the FBI, CIA and Sterling and then I saw them real ass suits in the yard when I got home. You saw that in the paper yesterday about Sterling wrapping up a 12 year investigation of that trucking company, with like 16 under cover agents, busted kilos if crack and pot. So if he would steak a place out for that long before he busted them and with all that time on his hands now why wouldn't he fuck with my head."

Red rolled her eyes in agreement "Yea, I hear ya,' I ain't sure what to think really. Just don't go doing nothing stupid and getting in trouble."

"I know baby I relize how insane it is, and it is probably, most likely my brain going haywire. But at the same time I got to know what's really going on." Shep stood and dove in the pool.

Red waited for him to surface as she walked down the shallow end steps "Of course you do."

He went back under water and came up facing her, not too close but close, they made deep eye contact for a butterfly moment. She fell away from him saying "Ya' know All Nights having a get together at his place off Hartly Bridge rd. tonight out at the field trailer."

Shep got excited " Well don't leave me in Dry Branch."

That night, at All Night's, most everybody there Shep knew. Deryl was there and Gabby, Barbra, Red, Al, and a few more that didn't make the finale cut of this autobiography. The stereo pumped out every thing from John Mellencamp, Nappy Roots, Boston, to Limp Biscuit.

There was a 10x10 tin shed in the back yard with a knee high bench along one of the walls lined with plastic half gallon containers. A five gallon pickle jar with three gallons of paint thinner and the organic base form of meth mixed in it looking like a clear liquid. All Night put a tube over into the mix and pumped air mixed with a white smoke of Hydrogen Chloride, from a bug sprayer containing sulfuric acid and table salt. It bubbled violently in the jar with every pump as the mixture in the jar formed methamphetamine salt and clouded up. Shep took the cloudy mixture and poured it into the coffee filters in the line of plastic containers. The meth stayed in the filter and the mixture was put back in the 5 gallon jar to be pumped with bubbles again.

When all was said and done All Night tossed Shep two eight balls of meth. Shep didn't complain, that was up to $700 worth, for 2 hours of work, start till clean up.

They took on different projects at the trailer that sat in the field for the next two days. Building a pump house over the well pump, a dog house, shampooed the carpet, washed Al's truck, organized all the stuff in All Night's work van, built small front porch on the trailer, etc.

Shep didn't hear the Brown Recluses the entire time. Red asked him several times if he had them nanobugs talking to him. The Recluses just listened, they figured it would really screw up the whole, we are really physically out here, thing if he was the only one to hear it with all those people as witness.

Chapter 15

A few nights after the party Shep found himself alone again, Across the driveway Deryl's house was empty and dimly lit by moon light. Sitting up in his bed by the light of his LED lantern reading an article in a Play Boy Magazine Shep's constant listing with all his attention made him hear nothing but silence every second that passed by. He had hung a blanket over the blinds for extra privacy.

Martin the CIA reminded the motel room of Fed's "Let's stick to the plan, from the Tabatha, in Savannah, he hasn't thought about it since the first night we heard him thinking, so it will be a out of no where surprise but something he will relate to strongly. It sounds like he has this nanotechnology thing figured out but he doesn't believe it, so lets don't blow our cover, we need him to think we are really out in that yard to scare him best." Like a movie director he clapped his hands and pointed to a 28 year old girl brown eyes , brown hair, blond streaks shoulder length, round face to mach her southern bell figure, from the DEA office, a new Recluse "action".

She spoke close to the microphone with the shoe box over it. Her voice a Alison Krauss whisper kinda' voice "Put that thing away."

Shep looked at the window to notice the blanket didn't quite cover the entire window, He did as he was told, then pushed the blanket and the blinds over to peek out, the closed window. He had found the window being let open made him nervous. As soon as he settled back down on the bed the voice spoke again. "Shep, I work at the DEA office and I am disappointed in you, when I over heard your name at the office it brought back memories of when my friend Tabatha told me years ago about how you left her on River Front Street in Savanna and a boat came down the river with a bunch of guys in it, they pulled over to the street and grabbed her in the early morning hours, you left her there with no way out Shep it's your fought she got raped."

Sterling spoke up "And we have special guest, come up to the window here and tell Shep how you feel sir."

Blair the FBI agent had the computer tablet, utilizing the voice masking technology. He activated the file with a mans voice he had went out of the way to obtain with phone taps. Sterling knew who Tabatha's dad was and knew he had went to the same church Shep had grew up in, Dry Branch ain't all that big. So it was not that much investigative work to get this scheme lined up.

Blair said in the mans voice through the tablet and Shep recognized it right off from growing up hearing it every Sunday morning and night at church. "Shep your going to have to pay for it. Tabatha's friend here told me what you did I never figured out why Tabatha's life went so wrong all of a sudden, it's your fought you left her on the streets and an eye for an eye and a tooth for a tooth, give me that bat Sterling, were going to bend you over tonight Shep."

The motel room was trying to cover all the laughs, and with great effort they held it down.

Shep was already explaining his innocents over the mind reading Bluetooth's hooked to the agents ears. Then he spoke out loud to the closed window, the speaker in the motel room and the moon lit, empty night. "In case there is somebody really out there, just incase, I was not the one that left her on the street, I was left with her and another girl, and I tried to stop her from getting on that boat but she told me and that other girl to mind our own business, and when she was brought back 45 minutes later she acted just fine."

"So now your calling my daughter a liar, lets go on in there and get him, I am not going to let him get away with this."

Shep got the two knives he had taped together pointing in opposite directions from a drawer and got the ax handle in hand. The Bluetooth ear buds told his thoughts in the weird computer sound, broken up but understandable enough, as "I need a gun, but that's why they fuck with me, if I had one they would stop and I got to know if this is real and they will give it away if they stay long enough. It's got to be Brian Sterling Wilson or hell what do I know it could be my boss from the mountains Brian Nelson and his work crew and that chick could be Merylin and or Shell in some crazy shit I haven't even came close to figuring out. I'm loosing my mind." Then he speaks to the window, "Y'all can try and come in on me if you want to but I'll fill you full of holes."

Knowing the answer Martin cleared his throat, getting the Fed's attention, then winked at them. In Tabatha's dad's voice he asked Shep. "What you got a gun in there man?"

"May be I do."

They messed with him for a while having to play like they had to hide from view when Shep would creep to the window to peek out. Then they had Sterling's brother, Sonny's voice walk up. "Sterling! You said you was going to leave him alone, what the hell is that bat for?"

Blair's voice came through the window loud an clear, so it sounded to Shep. "Damn, he snuck up on us." Sonny only lived 200 yards on down the road.

They played around with that for a wile. Shep was all into it, time melted away. He was looking for some kind of slip up to prove this was for real in technology or something. The Bluetooth's reminded them to be careful.

The morning was getting close. The motel room was getting tired The new girl (for name sake, Tiffina, a mix of Tiffany and Tina) had fit in just fine. She was sitting on the couch scrolling through all the voices that had been recorded. She decided to end it for the night. She really didn't think anyone would mind. She touched the file with Sonny's wife's voice in it. "Damn it Sonny, I just knew you had snuck up here to get you some meth, but now, I just got to know what the hell is going on?"

"I just came up here to make sure Shep was O.K., Sterling wants to stick a bat up Shep's ass."

"He want's to do what!?"

Sterling started explaining, but she cut him off, "Sterling you are one crazy son of a bitch. Sonny let's go you ain't got no business up here."

"Sterling said I had to stay and help."

She laughed "I hope he figures this out Sterling." Tiffina really did want Shep to figure out what was really going on. Sterling was thinking the same thing, although he had never told it. She added "Let's go Sonny, NOW!"

Shep slowly lifted the blinds up to look for them walking across Deryl's yard. He saw what could have been them (it had been a long night) but it could have been the last of the moon light casting shadows from the pecan trees. He heard the distant farewells from the Recluses standing as far from the microphone as they could get in the motel room, lingering their words. "Byyyyy Shep weeeeel bee baaack" "Yeaaa maaan your goinnnng tooo paaaaay for Tabbbathaas sake."

Chapter 16

The sun was setting on the woods surrounding Tiffany and Shane's house. The off white vinyl siding and green shudders gave it a relaxed homey look. The cement block that under pinned it and the large front porch gave it a sturdy look.

The burgundy Astro van pulled to a stop in gravel driveway. Tiffany had picked up Shep for a night of babysitting while her and Shane hit the town for some getaway.

Zachery at seven years of age by then just had to sit in the front passenger seat beside his mamma. Ship didn't mind taking the back seat. Marcus, Shep's son was 9 going on 16 was opening the back sliding door before the van had stopped good. Mathew at 3 years old sat in the very back seat with Shep in no hurry playing silly.

Tiffany called to deaf ears to Marcus and Zachery as they bolted for the house. "Thanks for helping mama with the groceries boys!"

Shep was unbuckling Mathew from his car seat, telling Tiffany "I'll get the groceries." Mathew grabbed a potato chip bag he had been snacking on. "I help you Shep."

"OK lil' buddy."

Tiffany was opening the back hatch of the van, ignoring Shep, and getting the four bags out. "I got it, shut the back for me."

With Mathew hot on her trail, the potato chip bag was over half as big as he was. They left Shep sitting in the van collecting his thoughts, wondering if he'd ever have it like Shane and Tiffany had it, kids, good jobs, nice house. He'd had it before he divorced her. After a minute he snapped back to his senses, picked up his book bag of clothes and exited the van.

After shutting the hatch he could barely hear a whisper and since he was looking at the vents that let air flow through the crawl space under the house his perception put the whisper from there.

Martin and Blair had been listing on the bug phones. Trying to sound like they were in the near by woods. The Bluetooth told them that Shep heard it from under the house instead. So they played on that, winging it.

Shep heard the whispering and laughing again as he was going up the front steps onto the porch. His common sense telling him that he may be a human bug for sure cause ain't no way anybody would crawl under a house and wait for them to get there, even if they had heard him talk about his destination all day. Or he thought maybe it was just shadow whispers his brain was tripping on.

He was putting cold stuff in the fridge, reaching up to open the freezer he spotted a five case of Raid spider foggers. He left the frozen foods on the floor. Tiffany walked into the kitchen as he was half way out the back door, leading to the back deck.

She asked, "What are you doing?"

"Killing Spiders." He couldn't let the coincidence of the foggers and the whisper of Brown Recluses under the house slip away.

She laughed "Spiders?"

Leaving Tiffany in the house, he jumped off the side of the back deck. Going to the scuttle hole, the only entrance leading to under the house crawl space. He said out loud "I don't know if anybody's under there or not, but better safe than sorry."

By then dusk was falling fast. The mind reading Bluetooth's of Blair and Martin talked Shep's thoughts. "Damn they could have crawled out while I was in the house, but hell nobody's under there, no matter how real this shit sounds." Blair and Martin decided to let it go before Shep decided not to react to any thing they said.

The scuttle hole door, a rectangle piece of plywood was already half way propped open when he set it to the side, to dark to see under there. Triggering the first bomb and strategically slung it as far as he could to the far end of the crawl space. He done the same with three more of them, covering the space evenly. There would be no escape from the fumes.

He put the scuttle hole door back in place, then wedged two logs from the fire wood pile on it, no escape.

Martin let out a very low cough as Shep went back into the house. Shep thought "I got to be the craziest son of a bitch in the world, cool though."

Tiffany was sitting under the cathedral ceiling in the den watching her recorded soaps on fast forward. "Did you see a spider?"

"Yea"

She stopped the soaps and turned off the TV "Are you alright?"

"Yea"

" You are looking crazier and crazier, you need to start eating, and give it a rest."

Shep didn't want to tell her he was up all nights waiting for the door to be kicked in. He had figured if they was real they could be really in the yard at night and talking to him through some kind of technology so it was hard to just go with gut instinct. It was taking it's toll. "I know, but don't worry bout them kid's being with me, I would die for them."

"I know." She added as if a after thought. "I heard your name and Deryl's at the court house today." Her job at the court house as a judges secretary put her in close ties with Drug Agents often.

Shep figured she was crying wolf to scare him, because she cared. He played along. "From who?"

"I can't say"

The back door opened, it was Shane. She sprung too her feet. "Hey pooh I'm gonna' warm up some left over's for supper."

He smiled. "Sounds good. Shep what's up man every thing going alright?"

"Mostly, how bout' ya' self?"

"Just switching back to 12 hour day shift sux. Tiffany you better get ready we got to meet them in an hour an a half and you know how long it takes you to do all that shit you do, like we going to Bunkingham Palace or something."

"K pooh" She through some stuff in the microwave and they disappeared to the back bedroom. Shep went the opposite way to Marcus's room.

An hour later they were rushing out the door. Shane asked about the spider and Shep said he had seen a huge one on the vent that go's under the house so he tossed a few bombs under there. Shane said the house was infested with them when they bought it that's why he got the foggers. Then he added as they got in his big tire 4x4 black Toyota truck. "Don't wait up for us…….. Never mind, you never sleep do you? Ha, ha." They left.

About two hours later Shep was pulling Mathew across the kitchen floor on a blanket. Mathew was carrying on, "I'm a Duke boy, Yee haw, The General Lee, yee haw."

Zackery had went to sleep in his room and Marcus was playing X-Box in his room.

"Shep you missed me" The whisper came from the kitchen window over the sink where Shep was closest too. "I had got out from under the house before you made it back there."

Then a voice that was loud and clear and unfamiliar, "Shep we got word of how you helped get all this Meth started around here. All our families have been infected by it."

Another voice spoke, very deep. "We're the Klan Shep. We Know about Tiffany and Shane buying phsudophed pills for you to cook. We have already took care of them at the end of the drive way."

Shep was standing at the window and it sounded so real but the height of the window kept him from seeing directly below it. He looked at the back door thinking of running for it to look into the back yard. But another voice kept him at the window. Mathew was standing beside him with his arms up wanting to see what had Shep's attention out the window.

A new voice said "We going to kill all of you and set you up like you did it and then committed suicide, Its extreme but in the end more lives will be better off, After they see what meth made you do to this family, you sick fuck, people will think long and hard about the dangers of meth."

Shep was thinking " But Tiffany and Shane have never got any pills for anybody and Klan or not killing the kids is ridiculous by any standard. So this is more bullshit." Zack had woke up, came out his room. Shep didn't notice until he heard the door of Marcus's room slam. Shep jumped out of his skin. Then with quick thinking an agent slammed his fist down on the microphone table not knowing what to expect. To Shep it sounded just like some body bumping into the outside of the house not far from the window. Like the slamming door had caused them to take off from under the window in such a hurry one of them bumped into the house.

All of it came too life when he heard that bump into the house. For sure and there was somebody out there, maybe not who they say they are but somebody was out there. One thing was for sure, he couldn't just run from window to window looking crazy all night so he had to go outside and face them.

He went to the utility room and got Shane's aluminum softball bat. Then gathered all the kids in the dark living room by the couch. No matter what he said he was doing he was going to sound a bit off so he just did the best he could do with it. "Boy's I think I saw a bear out there stowing the trash all over the yard, I'm going after it. I need y'all to stay rite here in case it tries to come in the house or something y'all can yell and I'll come running and kill it."

Mathew was looking in amazement. Marcus was thinking what Zack just went ahead and said. "Are you stupid or something?"

Shep smiled, "No I'm just crazy as a shit house rat, y'all just stay here, I got to piss before I go bear fighting." He went in the bathroom and shut the door. Taking a short straw and a bag of meth from his pocket he just dipped the straw in the bag and straight to his nose with it with a hard long snort. He flushed the toilet .

With the bat on his shoulder, going for the front door, he told Marcus to leave the big door open but lock the glass door when he went out after the bear. He got a nod from Marcus and out the door Shep went it was mighty dark out there standing on the front porch looking like a whacked out Mel Gibson with a bat. The taunts came clearly from the woods in front of him, down in the gully maybe.

The deep voice "You chicken shit you ain't coming out here."

Other voices "Shep we'll skin you alive." "cluck, cluck, cluck"

Shep sprang off the porch jumping the six steps, He ran full stride into the woods.

The motel room was ready for this they all had pieces of phone book paper in their hands. Waiting, grinning with anticipation.

Shep ducked under branches, tight grip on the bat and jumping big fallen tree limbs, zig-zaging his way through the dark woods, stopping near the bottom of the gully. Suddenly the woods came alive, the crushing of the paper next to the micro phone, in and out was to Shep leaves being rustled all around him, his eye's joined in the illusion as a voice said "GET HIM!" Shadow men came from behind trees over here then there making their way closer.

He went after them with the bat. The ping and pang on the trees echoed through the woods. His lungs bellowed in his madness. "I'll kill you all, stay away from those I love or you, you will all die!" The bat still going after the shadows darting around him. "I'll kill you!" Then he suddenly stopped and silence.

The motel room had froze in all of Shep's drama. That's what it was too a dramatic climax for the taking. They asked for it and he delivered.

Standing in the woods he recognized the sound of his heart thumping in his chest as he looked back up at the house, the kids. He broke into a trot out of the thick wooded gully. He reached the front door to see six eyes as big as saucers staring through the glass, obviously hearing the bat and bellows from the darkness. Seeing they were all accounted for Shep told them, "I got him, I just got to go secure the perimeter now, be right back."

Shep wouldn't be able to chill unless he checked the end of the driveway witch was to far away to see, so he sprinted bat in hand. Just as he suspected no sign of the threat that the voice had made about getting Tiffany and Shane. As he stood in the dirt road he could hear the computer generated four-wheeler sounds fade into the distance and the faint laughs of "We got him good that time." "He went slap nuts." "He almost hit me with that damn bat." faded till gone.

After Shep convinced Marcus to unlock the door, that every thing was cool, Mathew fell asleep on Shep's chest in the recliner watching TV. Zack fell asleep playing video games with Marcus whom finally dozed off.

The next morning Shane took Shep home to Dry Branch. He didn't speak of the crazy night before, they just talked about stuff. About 2 hours after Shep had been home the phone rang, It was Tiffany, "WHAT IN THE HELL DID YOU DO?!"

"Why?" is all Shep could think to say.

Shep didn't notice the night before what he was fixing to find out. Tiffany still angry but not yelling informed him. "Zachery said you went out in the woods with Shane's bat and was attacking somebody."

"It was a bear."

"OH, really now?"

"Well it might have been."

She started yelling again "Shane bought that bat for over 60 dollars just three weeks ago, and now it is dented flat in spots,!" She calmed back down a little. "Look until you chill the fuck out I am just going to have to get somebody to keep the kids."

"But" is all he got in. She hung her phone up.

Chapter 17

During the weeks following the Klan incident in the woods, Shep lost his job because Darby decided to dump his junk houses they were renovating and sold them all. Shep's dad gave him, his 73' Chevy light blue truck, a little rusty but the 350 engine, 4 barrel carb purrrd. It was a gift so he could have transportation to find another job and he searched diligently. Mean while he supported himself from meth sales.

The human bug theory was on his mind a lot. The way the voices/people sounded so real in his ears. He saw the absurdity in it, at the same time it sounded so real. Maybe Sterling was doing this as a radical way to scare him into sobriety. Maybe he wanted Shep to be a driving force in exterminating the world of nanobugs or maybe, maybe ,maybe.

Shep had been up all night, no voices had came that night. He was sitting in the den watching the news on CNN. It was Saturday morning and Ben, his cousin was in his room asleep and Trudy was in her room asleep. Unexpectedly at the den window he was sitting beside, the crunching of leaves then "Shep go to Tiffany's now."

First thought was, what if I don't and find out this was the opportunity to prove to himself that this is real or he was psychic, because what if something was wrong and he didn't go.

He didn't see telling his room mates about it, they may question his sanity. So he'd go to prove it to himself. He got dressed in some black work boots, jeans, and sleeveless T shirt and out the door he went. Seeing Grimsly's hatchet face, and skinny as a beanpole, looking like he hadn't seen a decent meal in a year, sitting in a lawn chair watching the grass grow by the morning sun in Deryl's yard gave him a witness. He approached Grimsly. "Hey bro' what's up?"

Grimsly shook his head, "Hell man I cain't call it."

"Have you seen anybody around the house over there?"

Grimsly grinned "Naw, Red told me you been tripping about some Fed's wanting to stick a bat up your ass."

Shep giggled "Something like that, I heard a voice walla'go tell me to go to Tiffany's, so I was thinking wellll….."

"So you want me to go with you?"

"I was just needing a witness, ya' know jus-in-case."

"I don't know or not, but I would not be surprised if you ain't on to something."

"Probably done lost my mind really though."

Grimsly sounded sincere adding "Don't go over there acting crazy."

"I ain't, I'll hollar at you later."

Blair and Martin were the only two messing with Shep that morning using their bug phones. After they gave the instructions to go to Tiffany's, they ate the free Howard Johnson Inn continental breakfast and just listened to Shep's brain sing Metallica songs in a computer voice. Shep had wired a CD, radio boom box into the trucks wiring.

20 minutes later he was sitting in Tiffany's driveway looking crazy as Hell, being the van and the truck was gone. But since he had done drove so far he decided to take a closer look. Standing on the front porch he opened the glass door to knock on the wood door.

Martin said into the bug phone "shhhh somebody's at the door."

Shep barely heard it and tried the door knob, it was not locked, so he pushed the door open fast. This caused the pressure in the house to change enough to cause a closed bed room door to sound as if it had been quietly closed. "Hello! Anybody here?" Making his way around through the kitchen and down the short hallway to the closed door of the back bedroom he stood holding his breath.

The whisper again "If he opens that door I'm going to blow his head off."

NOW I/Shep know you the reader are probably thinking who in the hell would believe their ears, and let me tell you I did not want to believe mine, I knew I should have not been reacting to things I couldn't see or that seemed out-rages. The things I heard were so real sounding, until you have experienced it, it is unbelievable. Also I needed to know if I may be a human bug or not, and if I didn't go along with it I would never catch them slipping, letting an opportunity to save the world pass by.

Instead of opening the door and highly unlikely but possibly getting his head blown off Shep had a better idea. He went to the den and clicked through the caller ID box till he located a familiar name that just happened to live down the road. "Hey man this is Tiffany's ex-husband, Shep…"

The red bearded 26 year old 250 pound redneck on the flip side of the phone recalled "Yea Shep what's been going on, ain't seen you in a while."

"Well I just stopped by over here at Tiffany's and nobody was home, there ain't no cars here, and I swear it sounded like somebody slammed a door in the house, nobody answered when I knocked so I came in to check things out and it sounds like somebody was moving around in the bed room, I think it may be a burglar in there."

"On the way." click

Two minutes later, Shep waiting on the front steps, a huge tire old truck was sitting in the driveway he had brought his pump shot gun with him. He pumped it "Point me in the general direction."

Shep went to telling the story again as they moved into the house, just the other side the thresh-hold the sound of cars pulling right up to the front door halted them. The neighbor informed Shep "Oh yea', I went ahead and called the sheriff."

In the yard sat two Deputy cars and two deputies, slightly over weight black hair they looked like brothers. The neighbor must have went to school with them the way they started caring on.

Then the attention turned to Shep. He went to telling the story again of how he ended up standing there looking crazy as hell once more. One of the deputies said he would check it out, so Shep led him to the hallway and pointed to the bedroom door. He told Shep to stay in the kitchen, then with his gun in one hand he turned the door knob just enough to unlatch the door, taking his gun in both hands he kicked the door open scanning the room with the gun. He informed his partner with a yell. "The bedrooms clear!"

Shep came into the bedroom to see the bathroom door shut. He pointed to it. The Deputy told him to stand outside in the hallway and went through the same motions as before. "The bathroom's clear!"

Shep investigated it and noticed the 2x2 window was open and had no screen on it. Rather than point that out Shep lied and said "Maybe I heard the back door shut or something, can we check the shed."

The Deputy did not hesitate "It's my job, that's what I do. So your Tiffany's ex?"

It wasn't a surprise that Tiffany had mentioned him. Her job at the court house put her and Shane on many of the deputies friends list, and Shane had grew up with a few of them in the county school system.

"Yea, guess y'all heard of me?"

"She's mention you."

"All good I hope."

"She's mentioned you."

Shep smiled, at that. They walked out the front door so he could let the other Deputy know what was up. He just nodded and kept on with his conversation with the neighbor. So just Shep and the one Deputy made way around to the back yard that was in-closed by a fence. Walking along outside the fence they could see the padlock on the shed door, but they continued walking a few more steps to see behind the shed. This put them at the tree line with a wooded valley with a creek at the bottom. The Deputy let his coworker, whom was out of site, know. "The shed's clear!"

As they stood at the tree line the Deputy was telling Shep that things looked OK…. But Shep's attention was drawn to the sound of the out of site creek down in the woods and a voice that tempted him. "When they leave we'll finish the job."

Shep didn't even think he just took off down into the wood s like a deer. "I'll be back." down at the creek he started walking, following it around toward the dirt road and the front of the house which was out of site. As he walked he started thinking he had done went way to far this time, the law, at her house, the neighbor, she is going to be pissed.

Blair played the sound of a 4-weeler pulling off just for fun. Shep noticed it and placed it on the old logging road that was on the far side of the creek. "Damn" Shep thought "They made their get away again."

To top it off as he made his way around the woods to the front side of the house Shane's dad pulled up in the yard after hearing the address on his police scanner, the other neighbors, next door happened to see the Deputy cars through the woods from their house, and made their way over, and Tiffany and her mama came up in separate cars, from the T-ball game they had been at. Luckily, Shane had took the kid's to Tasty Freeze.

Shep was surprised as a cat caught in a fan belt when he come out them woods to all them eyes staring right at him. He didn't show it one bit, he just walked straight to his truck opened the door, announced to the crowd, "The woods are clear!" climbed in and pulled off not making eye contact with none of em'. He was back in Dry Branch telling Grimsly all about it 20 minutes later.

Tiffina the Recluse had heard the whole thing go down on her bug phone as she sat around her place with nothing better to do. She texted Martin's phone. *never under estimate your opponent*

Tiffany was not happy.

Chapter 18

A few nights went by and nothing happened. Then one night Shep was being entertained by the Brown Recluses, they had lured him outside to the front yard. As he stood between the house and Hwy. 80, thinking maybe they are doing both, talking to my ears and really out here, two knives taped together in one hand and ax handle in the other, the midnight moonlight danced in the yard through the Pine-limbs over head, the shadows came to life all around him.

The sound of the slight wind, no one, but him, would have noticed filled his ears with doubt, on account he was listening to the shadows so hard.

The taunts of the Recluses moved in closer. "Shep there's spiders in the house, we jimmied the back door open swiftly and let our selves in."

Hearing and seeing he was surrounded, his get away became the Hwy. 80 to Gailu dr. They had cut him off from Deryl's physically and figuratively speaking. It was too many of them, flight seemed the only way to preserve his asses virginity.

Ax handle and knives in hand, he broke into a sprint across his yard, the driveway, and at a angle across Deryl's front yard under the pecan trees to the ditch, he jumped landing on the highway. Imagining himself with bionic powers, maybe caused by the nanobugs, putting one foot in front of the other, long strides, being careful not to stab himself with the knives, faster, faster. The Feds hot on his trail like a bunch of wild Indians with a baseball bat.

100 or so yards later he cut across a back yard that lead to his parents back yard, past the sliding glass doors of his parents bedroom porch. The Recluses had fell back, staying about 50 yards, or so it sounded, up the highway. Still at full speed he past the shed and the pool. The Bluetooth's of mind reading at the motel room told Shep's thoughts "What the fuck am I doing?"

It was not a thinking thing any more it was a feeling, a feeling that over-road his commonsense, it was so real. He stashed the knifes and the ax handle by tossing them into the utility room under the carport. The house door was locked he rang the doorbell. A minute later the carport light came on showing the bright whites of his eye's his pupils dilated to the max, his mom, seeing her 28 yr. old, she opened the door and he went with "I need to stay here tonight, somebody is messing with me up there."

Obviously she had done caught wind of Shep's state of mind, because she did not ask "Who?" Her face had a sudden horrified look upon it and she said in a sobbing voice "It's that stuff that meth, it's fried your brain!"

Shep calmly took that into consideration. "I don't know mama, there is something else going on."

She backed up a few steps and let him in. He stood in the living room, nicely furnished, neat and clean, with three full length widows looking out to the streetlight that lit up that portion of Gailu dr.. "I need to just stay here tonight."

His dad had heard every word from the bedroom. The heavy footsteps came down the hall toward Shep. Frank, the 55 year old triathlon competitor burst onto the scene fist balled up. He had never punched Shep but the night wasn't over, All Franks Baptist, was put on hold. "GOD DAMN IT SON It's that fucking DOPE it's done turned your brain to shit!"

Shep found some negotiation rite fast. "Just go up there and sneak up in the driveway and see if you see anybody if their ain't nobody there I swear I'll go get some help tomorrow, I don't know what is happening daddy but something is going on!"

Frank grabbed the keys off the key rack by the carport door and Shep and his mamma sat on the couch and watched him go to the stop sign and turn toward Shep's house. Shep could see the stop sign, he started thinking about the day Deseray and Shaky had dropped him off there over year and a half before.

His mama, Louise, took a deep breath. "You are ruining your life."

Shep thought to the Bluetooth's, which only excepted his strongest thoughts. The ones that would go to his voice box but he decided to keep to him self. "It's still better than smoking crack" But he said out loud, "I just…" that's all he said.

She didn't push it. His dad came hauling ass back to the house. He came in the door smiling and calmly hung the keys up. Shep didn't know what to make of this and it struck the Recluses, from Shep's thought's, just how twisted our perception can be. "He is in on it now, Sterling's done told him their plan of scaring me strait." This was over lapped with, "I got to get help, I am thinking some crazy shit."

Martin recalled the sliding glass doors in Frank and Louise's bedroom Shep had thought about as he was sprinting by them. He put the microphone close to the bed side table drawer and slowly opened and closed it, causing a sliding and latch sound. Shep looked back toward the direction of the bedroom. Tiffina took the microphone from martin and put it beside her butt as she sat down hard on the motel room bed.

Shep looked at his mama "Did you hear something?"

"No, I didn't hear something."

"It sounded like yall's glass doors, like somebody back there"

"Nobody's back there."

"Go look and see." Shep knew he was pushing it, but he had to because what if this was his chance to clear his sanity. If he could get his mama to go back there before his dad was able to let her in on the fact that Sterling was probably back there making sure he didn't tell Shep about him finding the Recluses in the yard......I guess you had to be there, but it all made since to Shep at the time.

"How do you know mama? Go look."

"No"

"Why, cause you scared?"

Frank had, had enough of that shit. "DAMN IT SON!" He stomped down the hall with Louise hot on his trail and slammed the bedroom door.

Shep debated on weather to go back up the road and take his chances with the spiders. He ended up just laying on their couch all night wide awake thinking.

Chapter 19

The morning after Shep sprinted into intervention, he sat in the waiting area of the emergency room with his parents. There was no conversation. Finally Shep was called to the back, he went alone. A Doctor of some kind came to the room. Shep gave him a very brief description of the voices at the window. The Doctor question if he was on drugs, Shep admitted he liked meth. The Doctor told Shep that he could send him to have a mental health evaluation, it was a three day process, it would be by Shep's on choice, so he could leave the mental hospital if he wanted to. Shep decided he would just go home after all he had his own place, he was 28, what could his dad do about it.

Last moment, Shep figured it was just three days, and he really didn't want to go back into the waiting area and face his mom and dad and probably have to walk 12 miles home, where he may get kicked out by Trudy's parents, because they owned the house Shep lived in and his parents had some church pull with them. They probably wouldn't want somebody living with their daughter that was being harassed by the CIA the FBI and the DEA.

Shep was led to another room with a dentist chair in it, minus the over head light, but it had straps on it to strap people down that were behaving violently. The window on the door was a bubble so those looking into the room could stick their head in the bubble and see all four corners of the room.

Locked in the room he laid on the chair and waited. It took about two minutes for Sterling and the DEA nark, Dumbass, whom were at the DEA office listening to Shep on Sterling's Bug phone, without the Bluetooth mind reading tech on, while they worked on plans for a drug sting they were doing that afternoon. Sterling turned the microphone on and being the only ones at the office put the bug phone in his office next to the door, shutting it, then went down the hallway as far as they could trying, trying to control their voices to give the illusion of an even greater distance. Dumbass impersonated Franks voice best he could. "Sterling! What are you doing here!"

Shep jumped to the window not being able to see far down the hallway due to the bubble window obstructing his view, he didn't expect to see anything, because he never saw anything, but it sounded as real as seeing it.

Sterling answered Dumbass's impersonation of Frank. "Frank I did not do this to Shep he did it to himself, we have been trying to scare him into acting right."

"Sterling how did you know he was at the hospital? We didn't tell anybody we was coming here, and now here you are coming from the back entrance, if we hadn't been back here to talk to the doctor we would have never seen you."

"I came to help him Frank I was going to tell the doctor to make sure they kept him at the Mental Hospital for a wile, The DEA is fixing to bust a few of his buddies and I don't want him caught up in it."

Frank's voice impersonation exploded "What are y'all up to, how the hell did you know to come here what did you do to my son,?!"

What was supposed to be the doctors voice, "Mr. Taylor calm down." Then really loud "Can I get some security in here?!"

Sterling with force, "Frank calm down, get your hand's off me, I'll arrest you!"

Shep's mom's voice was badly impersonated by Dumbass, "Frank, Frank, calm down!"

Shep looking out the window, the sound of the voices had captivated his attention.

Frank's voice insisted, "I know about it, Deryl told us he had done went crazy thinking he had some technology in him, that y'all had been listening to, he was right, that's the only way you would know he was here!"

"Sir, come with us, you must leave now!"

Sterling explained "Frank I didn't do this to him. I'm just trying to help him."

Louise begged "Come on Frank."

Frank's voice faded away. "I know Sterling he brought it on himself, I just don't want him to accidentally kill somebody because y'all are out in his yard at night, then he get life in prison, I love my son and what's this crap y'all put in him going to do to his body?"

The voice was almost out of hearing rang. "I know you do Frank, We were hiding behind Deryl's Shed last night when you pulled in the drive way................."

It was a long, long day in the small room he was locked in. That evening a van delivered him to Central State Mental Hospital. Shep got off the van in the parking lot as the security lights buzzed, starting their nightly shift. A big Castle like building, with 3 long rows of big bard widows, surrounded by trees and grass and other loony bin looking buildings, it was a big place.

He was admitted in by some very nice women, and taken to the third floor by a security guard. They got off the elevator facing a set of heavy steel doors. Shep asked, "So where am I?"

"This is the Powell building and this is Powell three east wing for the criminally insane."

Chapter 20

The criminally insane hall was lined with bed rooms no doors on them but nice beds with mattress on them. It smelled like a hospital and looked like one. It had been refurbished not so long ago. The hall led to a nurses station and a dayroom with nice cushiony couches, a big screen TV, coffee tables and pictures of flowers on the wall, one disproportioned white man stood, swaying, and rocking. A few young to old black and white men, that looked homeless sat around the room. To the right was a hall that led to another dayroom, the kitchen/dinning area and a smoking area that looked like a baseball dug out into the side of the building 3 stories high, looking out to creepy buildings grass and trees.

Shep didn't plan on getting used to it he figured three days and he was out of there. The first night was uneventful. The next day he spent getting blood work done and all that, he found out why the other men looked homeless when he was gave his way oversized, donated in 1970 something, slacks and shirt. The Shrink was some old man that seemed to barely speak English. He cut Shep off as he was telling his nanobug story, by insisting he had heard enough. He prescribed Shep some strong sedatives and antipsychotic meds, telling him it would take a week or two for them to work their magic.

That night after lights out the place got quiet. He had a room to himself. The Recluses had a plan, they decided, to act like the had cut a hole in the ventilation system in a nearby, unused portion of the building. They put the microphone in a 2 foot long piece of tin A/C duct and covered the end with tin foil. It worked, sounding to Shep like the real deal, but he knew there was not any body in that building talking to him, He listened as they told him all kinds of stuff was going on, bad stuff. The kids and Tiffany being in a wreck, in critical condition, his mom falling off a ladder trying to get some dishes out a cabinet. His cousin Ben being arrested for manslaughter, because he was DUI and ran over somebody. Just on and on they talked. Shep knew he was stuck there listening so he took it with a grain of salt.

Three days my ass. Shep was told he needed to be kept for observation the day's turned to weeks. The meds had such side effects that he started spitting them out. They didn't stop the voices in the vent's, that only spoke once in a while anyway so, the pills didn't change anything. After five days of taking them he couldn't deal with the anxiety, the shakes, the feeling of zombiefucation.

He was laid back on his bed one morning after breakfast, something he was not supposed to do, and the Feds still talking from the vent had his attention saying something about his son's brother Zack being ran over by Shane in the driveway. Shep was wandering if he was missing Kelly Rippa.

They ignored his thoughts continuing with the story of, locked Shane up he was DUI, then the voice in the vent said, with amazement, "Holy Shit,".

Shep noticed then the hustle and bustle of the hall had went quiet. The voices in the vent said no more. The hall sounded like it had been evacuated leaving only Shep. He went toward the day room to investigate, he found all eye's watching a plane burn in the side of a skyscraper, then as he watched another one hit. It was September the 11th, 2001. News of the pentagon being hit soon followed.

After the shock of what was going on eased, he wondered if his mind had subliminally noticed the hall going quiet and produced the "Holy Shit" before he noticed it or maybe that was his proof, but with conflict of knowing which, it was not proof.

Ideas of why this Bin Lauden would do such a thing as what they clamed he was responsible for, and why those places?, made Shep come up with some theories, not scenarios he had much faith in just what if's. What if our CIA had bugged Bin Lauden and was talking to him telling him to do things for America like it was Bin's God Alla or were ever he put his faith, and Bin wasn't buying it and knew it was the CIA. So he figured the most likely places was from the place with the best reception. On top of them tall buildings and at the headquarters of national defense, The Pentagon. Or maybe he had the technology to triangulate the source. But they couldn't read his mind because soon after he was wise to the bugs he went into a shielded cave deep in the earth and planned the attack. The emergency of 911 was nanobugs.

Highly unlikely but just as unlikely who would have thought those dollar bills could have been folded, by BIG coincidence, to form the fall of the twin towers in near exact replay and one for the Pentagon also. If you the reader has not seen this folding of the bills YOU TUBE it.

Shep was called to the counselors office, and told he had a warrant for his arrest for back child support. Tiffany had filed for it a week before Shep got locked up in this god forsaken place he was in, and he had been there for three months. The child support folks didn't care where Shep had been it was all up to a judge now and Shep being in the loony bin for, according to his doctors statement, was due to a lot of meth, was not going to look good at all.

It was a little over five months before Shep would leave the Hospital. He was spared going to jail thanks to loving family from far away. By that time the voices had faded away from the vents. It was not because of any med's, he always spit them back out. It seemed the time away from the meth must have done the trick.

Chapter 21

Shep had to wait a few days for his rescue. Sue, 28' a good looking, brown long hair, blue eyes, cute pug nose, ex-dancer, was taking him to South Carolina with her. Her mom was actually the one that paid off the child support under the condition he move up there with Sue and get a job. He had to give his pay check to her and she would send off the child support off and take care of all his living expenses. She had married a man with a lot of money and he was willing to give Shep a chance, and help out.

Sterling entered the motel room and faced the crew of Brown Recluses. "Blue hair today Tiffina?"

She brushed it from her eyes, it was a wig that made her look like an amine cartoon character. "Oh, you noticed." She grinned.

Sterling grabbed a chair and spun it around startling it backward, resting his arms on the back of it. "So what do we got going on?"

Martin stood up from the table and took a deep breath, "I called this meeting to inform everybody that there's going to be some changes." He leaned on the table with his fist. "I have to take the bug phones back. We are not the only ones listening to Shep and the powers that be said it's a security issue. Shep is guessing damn close to what is really going on and that's the next best thing to knowing. I ain't sure what he could do if he did know for a fact, except run around and make people think he is of a different reality, cause I don't see anybody believing him enough to do anything about it. But they want the bug phones back to tighten up the operation."

Prep asked, "I can't help wondering if Bin Laden was a human bug."

The FBI agent Blair shook his head. "Don't wander off too far on that and get lost looking for something you'll never know."

Martin pointed out. "As easy as it is to bug a human there ain't no telling how many they got. Hell, I don't know if I or all of us are one, I mean, how would they police us, make sure we ain't conspiring to tell the world about this and prove it. I have to admit I don't like this Big Brother shit, but it's my job it's what I do."

Prep joined in "It's what I do too, talk to a human bug"

Dumbass asked "Shep is going away to South Carolina, how are we going to play that out?"

Sterling gave his notion on the move. "I say we wing it like we been doing. It's crazy to spend time planning for something that has so many unknowns."

That made sense to the Spiders so Martin moved on to the next thing. "And we will be moving to a more secluded, secure spot. The location is being prepared now by those sworn to secrecy."

Tiffina mentioned, from no's where, "We got over 1000 sound effects on the tablet, I just happened to notice that the other day."

Martin smiled, "O.K. moving right on along, we got some Men In Black, no, no aliens, but if there was aliens that's what these men would do, since there is not, they will be coming to join us. It is training for them, I guess. I know we stopped entertaining Shep while he has been at the coo coo house. It was boring, we will come up with some good material now that he is getting out and we got all these brains with fresh ideas. We'll see if they can handle the pressure and responsibility we have to deal with on a daily bases around here."

That aroused a chuckle, and Prep said "I know that's right, the world is in the palm of my hand's, or it was till you took the bug phones. Now it's that microphone and tablet sitting on the table there."

Tiffina was trying to imagine the new place, having no idea of what to expect, and with more people in it. "How many MIB's will we be entertaining"

Martin had asked his higher ups the same thing for the same reason. "15 more men, so I hope the new place is roomy."

Deep inside the mountain, states away, the Brad Pitt looking scientist sat at his desk, reading about some organic chemistry stuff, listening to a speaker on his desk. "Make that 16, 16 men on the way."

Chapter 22

Sterling, Dumbass and Tiffina, back to her normal blond hair, met at the wildlife refuge near Macon . Their final destination being four acres' surrounded by 12 foot high fence topped with razor wire. They corralled at a steal gate while Sterling leaned out the window and entered the code, It slowly opened with the sound of a winding motor. The long drive way was lined with hard wood trees and fairly thick bush. From the out side the cabin greeted them with a full length front porch and the logs of the fairly nice size square building looked to be real logs. Probably the kind you order and they come pre cut numbered and ready to stack.

The one room cabin felt cozy, with a A/C unit, a kitchen in the corner, a long pick-nick table, three large plush couches, a mid-sized flat screen TV hung on the wall. No window's. A door in the back corner led to a bathroom complete with a shower.

The three laptop computers on the table were neatly wired together. Plus four wireless microphones, a speaker and a large black, metal box with an antenna wire that ran out side to a satellite dish, another wire left the box and hooked to a cable TV receptacle. Dumbass had already been there to be trained on the computers. He was the acting gadget guy at the DEA office. He would show the other agents how to operate it. One of the computers had a real time satellite imaging program on it. One of them kind you could nearly read the morning paper from space if some one was sitting on there deck reading it.

They fired up the nanobug application and Tiffina passed out some Bluetooth ear buds, turned the speaker and one of the microphones on and Shep was in mid thought coming over the Bluetooth in that computer mind reading voice. "… she wasn't my cousin, let me tell ya'…….." Then a voice came from the speaker on the table. "Mr. Shep she's not gonna' get here any faster with you sitting out here in the hall by the door. Go on in the dayroom and relax."

Shep stood up "I can't relax I am ready to……" The door buzzer buzzed, and clicked. The security guard that had shown Shep up to the third floor over five months ago stood smiling. "Man, you have a ride waiting on you down stairs."

In the elevator Shep told the security guard how the stay had done him good, how the voices that were messing with him seem to have faded away on their own. The guard told Shep that was good, rarely did he see people leave the hospital with out the same problems they had when they got there.

Sue had brought some clothes in for him to change into, and the rest of his cloths, she had in the trunk. They would be going straight to South Carolina, no detour to Dry Branch. Shep was cool with that. That was a lie.

The burgundy box shaped diesel Volvo sat under partly cloudy skies. Shep opened his door and sat down, every thing was cool, he shut his door. While Sue was fumbling with the key's she had only looked the drivers side door, Shep's world was shocked.

Sterling jumped off the couch and to the table with the microphone on it, he spoke close to the mic. "Shep, you know who this is don't you?"

This being the first time a voice had no regard about being camouflaged in a vent or the woods or outside in the dark, this voice was sitting in the seat behind him. Sue was just about to open her door, Shep in a low calm voice answered, "Sterling Fucking Wilson."

"I could be, we fixing to give you HELL BOY!"

Sue sat down. "Are you alright?"

"Yea, all good just getting used to the outside world." Is what he said. He was thinking how in the hell did they go away, then come back, this is crazy, I haven't even done any meth in over five months and that was the loudest most in my face voice they have done so far. Not telling Sue seemed like the best idea. She had told him while he was signing paper work etc. all about the big house and the pond right outside the door among other stuff and he didn't see scaring her out of the deal by acting like what had got him there in the first place.

Sterling was still at it nonstop. "Boy, you think you can run and hide from us? Shep this has only just began, we are either going to kill you or make you stronger. I am sick of playing around with you, your folks raised you good and you throw it all away on drugs. Shep lets just see how long you can put up with non stop.............." Sterling at the time wasn't sure how long he, himself would last, it was a last second decision to start talking non stop, and he wasn't even thinking if the rest of the gang was willing to jump on the crazy train.

Tiffina and Dumbass sat looking at Sterling waiting for there chance to put there 2 cents in, but Sterling was on a role throwing every thing and the Bible at Shep. Talking heart to bug one minute, cussing him for all he was worth the next. Sterling knew Shep could not talk out loud, with Sue sitting there, but he kept drilling Shep with questions, "What the hell was you thinking, just why Shep just why..................An hour went by and a few miles, Sterling's voice started getting horse.

Tiffina and Dumbass joined in the stoning. It was non stop preaching and guilt trips Shep should be on because of this and that, and a lot of lies about people getting killed or busted or raped. The spiders in his ears didn't care if he believed the lies it was just there imagination running wild, it was something to say instead of saying the same thing over and over and maybe it was tearing Shep down little bit by little bit so in the end he would kill himself or become callous and stronger. They had no idea how long nonstop would be.

Sue was talking about her three kids and her mama and her husband, Will who was about twenty years her elder but he had a lot of money and after she told Shep how he got the money, Shep judged him to be smart for starting his own insurance company in the tax free islands where a lot of crooks do, so Shep was suspicious. He was a doctor of some sorts and paid his own insurance to his own insurance company tax free. Supposedly he was his only account so no one got hurt when he retired and closed the insurance company. But shady for using Sue as a mule to bring it to the states tax free. Maybe she should have worked out a lump some deal for transport and ditched his ass.

Tiffina told Shep they had relocated to a protected area that was teaming with real wildlife, She said she felt like she was at a mountain cabin and she could smell the log walls, and only 20 minutes from home. From that Shep painted a pic of a national wildlife refuge etc.

Sue and Shep rode with silence between them. It was his fought he wanted to have a conversation with her but he felt like he didn't want to miss what the Recluses said. What if they told him something that made them real then would not repeat it because he was talking. It was distracting not being in his mind. It was all in his ears just like they sat in the car with him.

Five hours later that seemed to be ten to Shep, they had not stopped talking for three seconds, the Volvo pulled in a dirt driveway that passed by a three acre pond on the left, woods all around except for a good size yard to the back of the two story house. The house built with stone walls, halfway up then a barn red lap board siding to the nearly flat roof with just enough slant so the water would know which way to go. She pulled to the back of the house and parked, giving a view of the pond in front of them and the house to the left. Two doors on that side of the house one that entered into a hallway and sliding glass doors that went to the kitchen. At the glass doors stood Jessica, 12 big blue eyes and Shep happened to notice she would not need breast implants when she got older. She was pretty, favored her mom, Buddy 10 built like a bean pole with huge blue eyes, Katelyn 5 was skinny, blue eyes, long brown hair, pretty, and looked like she may just as well wear jeans and T-shirt to church cause you can't get dresses dirty.

Shep greeted the kids with hugs to the steady talking in his ears, saying they had some relief on the way. He met Will, who was nice looking, and very welcoming. Shep felt odd, he wanted to talk and hang out with the family but the voices were so distracting that even when he was paying attention to what they where saying he felt like he looked like he was lost. He didn't have much to say anyway he had been cut off from the outside world over 5 months and there just ain't much to say about life in the loony bin.

Each Crown Victorian entered the gated driveway with the head lights on. Ten of them parked tightly in the area in front of the cabin. Fifteen slightly different men between ages 25 and 35 wearing jeans to slacks, T-shirts to casual button downs got out the cars and waited for Martin, Blair, and Prep, who had got there moments before, to fill them in.

Sterling was telling Shep all about how the church Shep grew up in had some men on the way to help the Recluses…then said "Tell him all about it Barthalamule." and pointed to Dumbass as Sterling himself went out the door to the front porch.

Sterling left the door open and stood on the porch telling the new arrivals, "About time I got some relief."

Prep question him "How hard can it be?"

Tiffina had just stepped out the door. "Sterling started a new game."

Blair took to introducing everybody as best he could. "This is Sterling and Tiffina and that one in there babbling on is Dumbass, and this is the Men In Black." Blair noticed the look of disappointment on Tiffina's and Sterling's faces, adding, "I know, right, I felt the same way. Who would ever guess that the MIB's dressed like normal folks."

Martin asked, "So what's up with the new game?"

Tiffina about faced and went back inside. "Tell them about the new game Sterling."

Sterling thought on it a second. "I figured we could do it non stop till we kill him or make him stronger."

Prep looked confused. "We pretty much already listen to him 24/7"

Martin went in the cabin. "He means talk." he liked the idea mostly because he saw it as a test of who could last longer Shep or the Recluses and the MIB's.

Blair looked at the crowd of new men that thought they new what was going on but was not sure. He explained, "Looks like we will be splitting up into shifts after tonight, but for now lets go in there let you get a feel for it and till dawn we shall give THIS HUMANBUG HELL! He enjoyed putting the theatrics on the end.

Shep heard "……THIS HUMANBUG HELL!" that's when the voices started to slowly increase in number and volume. As Sue was showing him his up stairs room, which was Katelyn's room, she would be staying in Jessica's room now, the pinkness of it was overwhelming. The voices let him know that thing's had taken a turn for the worst. He tried to act like every thing was good, but by the way Sue kept asking if something was wrong he knew that acting was not going to get him through this.

He laid in the dark, silent room thoughts of worry overwhelmed him, would this last the rest of his life if he lived a long one, or maybe it's just a phase, Surly they can't go on long. They did stop talking the last three weeks at the hospital, why would they come back when he was on his way to a new and potentially better life.

The Agents carried on all Night putting them selves on the roof of Sue's. Adding some sound effects by wrapping the microphone in a towel and placing it under the table. They would pound there fist with a towel wrapped around it to make sounds of stomping around up there. They made up stories of Will being in on it and Sue being blackmailed to keep her mouth shut. Stories of Will forcing him self on Jessica, And a lot of yelling and chanting, "SHEP YOU WILL NEVER MAKE IT!" Then they would all say over and over, things like. "SUICIDE SHEP, SUICIDE SHEP, SUICIDE SHEP!" Prep and Dumbass made a big deal about a amplifier for Shep's nano-hertz radio waves that was being put on the roof as they spoke and they argued whether it was done rite, but it looked just like a shingle so how wrong could it be done. They all put bets on how long Shep would last, asking him for the inside scoop. He didn't know.

On and on all night, not in his head but real in his ears. It is hard to believe some could find enough shit to throw non stop for that long. On the other side, even if it is all in ones brain, that brain has done it, so I suppose several real people could do it. Just before noon the next day they slowly dwindled down to 4 voices that were unfamiliar to him but they just kept talking to Shep,Shep,Shep,Shep non stop. They said his name to him at the beginning of almost every thing they said. It was a torture technique to hold his attention just as close as possible, engulfing him in the madness. He didn't have any faith in the super natural, so figuratively speaking he decided if he let them kill him they would be his demons. If he used them to make him stronger they would be his angels.

Chapter 23

Will, Sue's husband, had an office in town from where he was working on his next big thing. Surfing the internet to find investors for a book he was writing. A safety standards, based on federal guidelines, for medical equipment, book. He had made over a million bucks with his insurance company scheme and Shep had a feeling this new venture was about as legal as the last, but kept his feelings to himself, and the Recluses, it gave them something to talk about.

Shep didn't see how it was the year of 2001 and a book of this nature, if needed, wasn't already out there. Will had came home for lunch that first day Shep was there and was telling him about it. He said he had raised so many thousands of dollars from investors already. Shep thought to the Recluses unknowingly, "If I heard my granddaddy, Walter Hortman, say it once I heard it a hundred times more, "There's a sucker born every minute.""

By 3:00 pm the voices had been talking for 24 hours nonstop. The four doing the talking had Prep as a coach of sorts, filling them in on Shep's past, giving them relevant things to talk and yell about. They used sound effects off the computer, with over 1000 to choose from. Shep could hear them in 3-D. The agents experimented by doing things like using all four microphones at the same time. Putting one in the cabinet, one on the far side of the room, one outside the front door, and talking directly into one, caused the illusion of being surrounded in Shep's ears. The agents figured they would be doing this shift work of non-stop talking for days maybe weeks, before some unforeseeable reason brought it to a halt. Like how much man power was the powers that be willing to put on a human bug that was no more than an unimportant young man from Dry Branch, Georgia.

Shep favored thinking that his brain had gone haywire and this may be a rest of his life thing or maybe they would stop just as quick as they started from scratch when he shut the Volvo door, and that could happen any minute now. He still couldn't help entertaining the conspiracy theory of being nanobugged. That's how he treated them as he whispered to them when he was alone. He knew better than to fight / argue with them no matter how hard they tried to push him into it. Misery loves company, so he kept a phrase he had coined at the rehab in Helen, years ago when this story started, "You got to take the good with the bad and the ugly and do the best you can with it." He tried to act as if all was well the rest of the day.

The Recluses had changed shifts. They did not hide the fact of it. "Shift change Shep, bout time, Yea Shep after this 30 minute lay over to bring the fresh crew up to par we got the next 4 days off till we have to be here again and still get a weeks pay, It's worth it Shep. "Yea Shep, if you last that long." "We here now Shep and if you think that last shit was tough way to you get a load of us………….." It was a long night he didn't sleep a wink.

Another shift of Fed's had his attention at the kitchen table the next day. Sue was cooking supper talking about taking Shep job hunting the next day. He decided to go ahead and spill the bean's, seeing how's it sounded like the voices were in it for the long hall. Telling her from the start of the recipe seemed to be the best way. The agent's kept talking but listened to the story as well. He told the story quick as possible, leaving out all the unnecessary detail. She knew Sterling from both being raised on Gailu dr.. Her brother was the bartender at the 38 Special concert the night Shep saw Martin and Blair in the yard, so he gave some detail of the nanobugged theory.

She had to be at the end of the driveway to get the kids off the School bus in a little while. After he got to the point of the matter, that being the voices talking to him from the time she picked him up till now, three days later. She said with nervousness "I did not realize it was that bad. Well, just ignore them. It's just your own brain talking to itself."

He pointed out that them talking in 3-D made ignoring impossible to do, but not to worry about him getting a job, a deal was a deal. He had no intention of going back to Dry Branch and end up sticking his aunt with the child support bill.

They all sat at the table for dinner and Will directed the conversation to the day's events of school work and such. The spiders just kept talking. They would comment on things that were said at the table by the family and some times go out in left field on their own subjects. Shep was torn between the two worlds, a larger piece of him fell to the voices. He made up for it by shaking his head as if he was paying attention to the table, laughing when the table laughed, and smiling if they smiled.

At the cabin, they had been careful not to give away the mind reading technology. Doing so may cause Shep to disregard the whole human bug theory, and that would make their games be far less entertaining for the all. They used it to their advantage also by hearing where Shep's thoughts were and if he went astray from their constant babble, he could quickly be herded back.

Chapter 24

Sue, Shep and Will sat, out the side door of the house, on the deck, in the evening, at a black iron table with an umbrella in the middle. The pond gave a nice view.

Will had been a general family doctor, using his expertise to look up something on the internet about Shep's condition was the subject on the table. Shep got the feeling Sue had told him about the new voices and the human bug theory.

The Recluses still talking for over three days now, started giving all kinds of views on Shep's situation. Will with his elbows on the table touched his finger tips together in from of his face, as if the all knowing authority on the subject. "The mind is a technical thing, and some things can cause it to warp. Those chemicals that you used to make meth have caused what is known as Psychosis.

Shep had done his homework and already ruled out that. "I understand the brain pretty well. It's the firing of neurons, the chemicals that are the keys to our emotion and thought causing a complex transfer of electrons across the web of a nervous system that is what we are."

Sue was sitting with a smile, eyes wide open and perfect posture. She looked as if she was surprised. Maybe it was because, Will didn't like his authority being questioned.

Will went on with his diagnoses with a bit of insistence in his voice, picking up a stack of paper he had printed out, tossing it over to Shep. "The bottom line is, It's the drug and the chemicals you are using to make it, causing you to hear things that aren't there."

Shep thought of all the people he knew that did the same meth he had done. They had their shadow men sightings and occasional shadow voices after being awake for a few days, but not one of them was experiencing what he was. He took in to consideration that human chemistry is slightly different person to person. This seemed way to drastic to be explained away on individualality.

The voices had input. "Ya' know Shep, you should stand up and bitch slap that mother fucker." "Yea Shep, he is already telling you not to eat between meals, like he's your daddy." "Shep you in a mess man, you got to live with that prick, and deal with us and keep a job." "Shep, bet you wished you had some meth to help you keep going."

That meth part was probably the most sensible thing he had heard them say yet. He explained to Will. "I know everybody's chemical make up is different, things can cause reactions in me like no one else. But I've been away from meth over five months and they just started to talk nonstop three days ago. That is what leads me to believe it may be a condition I was born to have, skitzo. On the other hand I have read that like 90% have skitzos show it before age 20, and it's virtually unheard of starting after age 25, and I am 29. So I know that it's hard to grasp, but when I mix the CIA, the FBI, and the DEA who were all really investigating the house I lived in because our cousin put in an application to work in Russia at the U.S. embassy, when I add it all up with the way the voices have evolved, like they had stopped talking the last three weeks at the mental hospital, then all of a sudden blasted into 24/7 when I sat down in the car to come here. When I take every thing into account I can't help entertaining the idea that I may be a human bug, a walking walky-talky."

Will looked at Sue. " The CIA and the FBI?" She must have left that part out when she told him Shep was shot-out.

Will shook his head with a 'I don't know what to do' shrug and Sue broke her silence. "Are you going to be able to work so I can mail off your child support and you can pay my mom back?"

"Oh yea I got it, a deal's a deal. It will be best if I have something to do, like a job, they already are dragging me down with this non-stop shit they talk, me feeling like I have a purpose will help me deal with them."

Will popped the question. "What are they saying right now?"

They had been talking and yelling about Shep never making it with them talking to him, how they would do everything to bring him to his demise, for one reason above all, because they had cash bets on his head. After Will showed interest one of them blurted out, "Tell him we are talking about you wanting to bang your fine ass cousin. I saw her on this satellite imaging we got she is fine Shep."

Instead of answering Will with that he went with the part about the bet's on his head."

Will smiled real big and raised his eyebrows. " I'm going to let you handle this Sue, I'm going to bed now." he started in the house.

Shep let him know, "I appreciate every thing you and Sue are doing for me man. I'm going to hold up my end of it."

He turned and looked at Sue. "That's what family's for."

Sue grinned and turned her attention to Shep. "Me and you are going to leave early in the morning and go to some temp agencies and get you a job."

"Sounds good."

She pointed out a trail that went back in the woods and ended on the far side of the pond, in the driveway near the road.

"How long is it you reckon?"

"Will said he walked it off to be about two miles."

" I think I'll take up jogging, it will do me good."

The voices had been, what sounded like yelling from the other side of the pond. They did it by using the sound effects on the computer to add a slight echo to their voice. One of them started hollering "RUN FORREST RUN, RUN FORREST!"

Shep started to laugh at his whole situation, it quickly turned to a "Damn!", of what am I going to do.

Sue was standing in the doorway looking at him. "What?"

He told her about the Forrest Gump reference, as another voice who had lost the echo effect and was next to Shep said "Shep you go back there in them woods jogging and it's going to be more like the movie Deliverance with this baseball bat, squeal, squeal, like a pig Shep." He wanted Sue to have a better idea of what he was dealing with so he told her about it too.

She added her joke in. "You ain't going to go Texas Chain Saw Massacre on us are you?"

"Hell no. I've been thinking about saving the world from big brothers nanobugs, weather I'm a human bug or not. Because one day if not already the nanobug technology will be out there and if it's not kept under lock and key it will threaten our freedom."

All Shep got from her was, "As long as you get a job and a cigarette and a light." She went inside. He walked down to the dock on the pond and smoked whispering to the Recluses in conversation about all that was going on. Then he went to bed, trying not to whisper answers to stupid questions but it only agitated them till he whispered then they would start on some other bullshit questions. Shep knew he had the disadvantage.

The job searching the next day was cool because he was with Sue and they had been close friends before kids turn into something like grown ups and move away from each other making their own way. It sucked too, Shep hated filling out applications writing the same thing over and over, possibly wasting his time. Most places a résumé just ain't enough. The voices didn't make things any easier.

He was ready to take that jog when he got home. It turned out to be a run, the Recluses, gave the story of two places at once, in his ears and in the woods, they had decided to send a few agents up there with him. Just incase an emergency happened and they needed to be on the scene to do a cover up operation. It wasn't true, but the real sound of foot stomps covertly running up behind you wearing some military camo, that was better than the real thing, makes people run faster whether they want to believe it or not. Put a bat in one of their hands and Shep don't even take the time to look back. It got his adrenaline pumping so he liked it, kinda' like meth and he would do it again.

Chapter 25

"Damn it Shep, only three days after you put in those applications and your walking in to your new job." "Hey Shep when I was in high school I did a lot of what your fixing to try to do." "Man, Shep I am glad you got a job. Talking to you all night while you lay in your bed and whisper about your days gone by and dreams of the new life you would have if only we would stop talking was OK the first time I heard it, but I was not looking forward to it a second go around." "Sorry I'm late men what did I miss? I met a girl at the bar here in Macon Shep. It was hard to leave her by herself at the motel room." "Big Shep a Big K-Mart man, stock boy, on the graveyard shift, man I hate it for ya'."...............

Shep had been thinking some meth would sure be good to get him off to a good start at his new job, being he had only nodded out a few times since they started talking 24/7 the day he left the mental hospital. He had not said it out loud knowing it would only make them more agitated. They had been careful not to reveal the computer voice of the mind reading technology they had been listing too, so although they commented on meth quite a bit it was always when it was further from his mind. Fucking with him in this way was to make him get used to thinking about meth and not having it, and it was a way to break some of the boredom of subjects when they had became to lax. Shep whispered as he took a leak alone in the bathroom. "If I could lift a bunch of psuedofed pills and make a big ol' batch maybe I could get used to this, I am drained and ain't even started." And the frenzy began.

Over the years in high school and between other jobs Shep had worked as stock boy in a number of places. Starting when he filled Hurley

Kelly's shoes at the store. Things had changed from those days of ticker taping each item with a price sticker. He had changed with it in the corporate world of learning how to scan under stocked items and upload to the computers, but starting at the bottom was where he was now. On the real, he always hated stocking shelves and he had got stuck doing all the small items, toothpaste, band-aids type stuff and then over to Tylenol etc.

"Shep this dose not go here it go's down there." "It goes on another isle man." "If I was you Shep I would push that pallet jack back to the loading dock and turn in my name tag and my vest."

Shep corrected, "I have a cart not a pallet jack."

The men sitting around the microphones quietly high fived the talker for the mind reading cover up, of Shep thinking, "Damn cart to small for all this........."

"Shep, I like the way you talk to yourself when you do this it sounds like your talking to us." "Shep, that is not the kind of deodorant I wear so take it all off the shelf, do the world a favor, that shit sux.".........

Shep recalled under his breath at the insanity. "I guess that bit about not talking to me at work was a lie.".......................

"Shep, Sue was killed in a wreck on her way home. She will not be picking you up."

He was kinda' used to this kind of talk they had been doing it all along. It did make him worry, but he knew if something like that had happened there was nothing he could do about it. From another perspective it bothered him to think if he did call and something of the nature had happened and he pointed it out to another party that he knew before he could have known any other way, it would raise question that either he was a human bug or had ESP. He had checked on a few things on the sly, to date, nothing panned out..

On his third night into his new job he was on break. He fired up a smoke just outside the front entrance, engaged in conversation with a young man that worked stock also. They had already had a few, nice weather conversations.

Shep decided to tell the coworker, the human bug theory. The reply to his five minute spill on this radical true to life, world altering, situation from the guy was an unemotional, "really." flipping his cigarette butt into the parking lot he walked back into Big-K.

Shep got the feeling he had just shot himself in the foot, but then why would that guy tell the boss about Shep's instability? But then again..........

The next day Sue came up stairs to Shep's room and woke him up. "Hey, do you want to come down and eat lunch with me?"

He felt like he had only nodded off ten minutes before. He decided quickly that he would join her, his other option was to lay there and listen to the agents going off like Marine drill instructors motivating him to start his day.

Over tuna fish on toast the two cousins spoke of the smell of pot that was in the air. She insisted that she would not share, on the grounds that Will, who did not smoke pot, said it may make the voices in his head worse. Shep argued he did not see how they could get any worse. He normally would not even care to smoke it. She kept it away from Shep his entire stay.

The phone rang, just in time to drive the final nail into Shep's hand and crucify his pot argument. She answered it, and past it to Shep. It was the temp agency letting him know that he was no longer needed at K-mart, He asked if there was any other openings he could start today. They told him basically, "Don't call us we'll call you."

Sue had the Recluses backing her up, "Seeeeee good thing you don't smoke pot you wouldn't pass a drug test now that you need another job."

Shep told her why he thought he got canned. She wished he hadn't had done that. Shep got dressed, no need for a jacket it was barely warm out, and they were going to town riding a Billy goat leading a hound. He showed his face at a few temp agencies he had already been too and he added another.

There was a call message waiting for him by the time they got home. The next day Shep was the new stocker at Wal-Mart. He had lucked up and got the cereal and not so tedious other items. It really was not any better, them voices in his ears just kept on and on and on. He questioned if that was proof they were just voices from his own brain who would talk to somebody non stop?.......As he pointed out to himself, it could be a lot more Recluses than I think and even with not many they can work 1 day a week and using that voice masking technology one guy could talk 20 minutes at a time and sound like a party of four then wait his turn to talk again so just for part of 8 hours 1 day a week and get paid a full week, not really a bad deal. BUT what do I know but a lot of guessing.

The third night of stocking at Wal-Mart was over. Listening to Tiffina tell him "great job". She had been gone five days. Having her as one of the talkers in his ear the night before was the best of a bad situation. She was helpful with positive statements.

He sat on a bench in front of the store to wait on Sue to pick him up. Sometimes she was waiting on him. Watching the seagull looking birds pick at the stuff that looked like food around the parking lot, he disregarded, best he could, all the trash the agents had been tossing into his head about all kinds of shit. In the near distance the sound of a Harley Davidson type motorcycle seemed to be coming closer. Till it sounded as if it should be in the parking lot, then it shut off. Shep saw nothing of the sort.

Tiffina's voice said "Shep be back in a sec., I got to go see who this is." She went out on the porch of the cabin. At the bottom of the steps was a medium built, leather jacketed, biker booted, faded jeans, man, removing his helmet. Standing beside a motorcycle with a frame made of chrome bones the wheel rims, curved chrome lighting bolts, and a chrome skull with a headlight fixed in it's wide open mouth.

The voices had actually got quite, they all followed Tiffina out to see what was out there. Tiffina was the first to return. "Shep it's Brad Pitt out there on one bad ass scooter." She went back outside.

The Brad Pitt look alike approached the group of Recluses on the porch. "Howdy, I'm looking for Martin and Blair." He flashed a government ID.

Tiffina ignored the intro. "I like your scooter."

The scientist from the lab inside the mountain continued to make himself at home, walking in the cabin taking it all in. "So is that Shep sitting on the table. "I bet he's glad I pulled up gave him a momentary laps of peace."

Shep sitting on the bench said out loud over the speaker on the table, "Short lived."

One of the agents, walking over to the microphone exclaimed. "Shep don't you get used to that! What the fuck are you doing right now Shep?"

"Watching them seagulls bro."

Another agent joined in "Shep, those seagulls are watching you. See Shep like I told you this morning, you never know when we are watching."

Shep heard the scientist. "Shep, I came all the way from a place that dose not exist. It's carved into a mountain, that's were I helped make that technology in them birds and that nano-shit that's in you. I been keeping tabs on all this and when I found out they had bets on the duration of your life span I just had to come lay my money on the beryl head."

Shep was sitting alone so he just blurted out, "The odds are in your favor either way you call it. So tell me about this scooter Tiffina done got her panties all in a wad about."

"Man, the bone frame is steel, chromed covered, the head light is a genuine human skull dipped in chrome the lighting bolt rims are like wise.

"Cool"

Tiffina and Scooter went back out on the porch and the other agents had their imaginations cranked up and went to telling Shep all kinds of lies about the new revelation.

Sue came slowly across the parking lot in the burgundy Volvo. Shep plopped down in the seat. The agents heard Sue's voice over the speaker, cause, in case you forgot that's one of the things the nanobugs in Shep can do, that's how they hear him talk out loud, the same way they hear around him. Sue's voice said. "So how was your night of putting shit on a shelf ?"

Shep tried to sound enthused "Spectacular."

Sue hopingly asked "Did they quit talking?"

Shep dittoed the voices. "Not a chance." Then he calmly added "In fact they may have just multiplied by one. Which technically that would still be the same number and may still hold true but it seems they have additioned by one."

Sue went, "oh"

Shep continued making small talk while the voices simultaneously raised hell. Talking to Sue on the way home felt good. The voices had really engulfed him.

Martin and Blair arrived at the cabin to meet with scooter, parking their blue Crown Vic next to the steps by the bike. After the "good to see ya's," they got down to business. Scooter had brought some experimental technology. He explained it to Martin, Blair, and Tiffina, "What I have back at my apartment in Macon, I think I'm going to stick around for a minute, shame I got to hide my bike, now that we told Shep what it looks like. Can't have witnesses by chance seeing it and collaborating his story. Well, anyway I have some kinda' experiment for Shep to try on."

Tiffina pointed out. "If it goes over his head he probably done tried it on, to block these signals, he had read that pine straw will block some signals that steel don't so he went for a walk the other day back to the woods and there he was a grown man standing in the woods holding a big ball of pine straw on top of his head. The guys working that day said they don't know who was laughing more them or Shep."

Scooter smiled "Damn, good try, nano hertz are hard to stop. But no this is called the copy-catter point one. That's all I can say about it at this time."

Mean while back at the pond in Sue's yard Shep was casting and reeling. He never had cared much for looking at a cork, so bass it was, and he was getting some good bite's. The Recluses seemed so human as he caught a fish and reeled it in they did their job and pulled for the fish. Pulling for Shep was not what they intended to sound as if they were doing. Then when the fish got off the hook before it reached shore three of them slipped before they caught them selves. It was the clear sound of disappointment in there voice that made it so human " Damn, Damn Shep it got away, you almost had him, damn it sure looked like you had him from this satellite we're watching you on................................"

Chapter 26

Scooter didn't like the motorcycle being taken out of the picture but it was a matter of national security now. He was driving a mid sized rental car when he showed back up at the cabin two days after his first visit. Dumbass and the other Recluses on shift had been expecting him with some curiosity. They found some disappointment in the absence of the skull headlight.

Scooter brought in a thing that looked like a VCR, sitting it on the picnic table with the computers, except where the cassette would go he inserted another box, explaining as he terminated a group of wires from here to there. "This will be known as the copy-catter experiment........(He typed on the keyboard) point one. And that's all I can say about that."

Leaving Shep and the crew to discuss theoretically what copy-catter meant, Scooter with a Bluetooth of Shep's thoughts on his ear, laid back on one of the couches, hands behind his head. While listening to the shenanigans, he reflected on the copy-catter. He didn't tell them the purpose of the box, not wanting to influence the way things are said. It needed to be natural to be most effective. He realized that it would get better results if he broadened the subjects. Why not unleash the beast? It didn't matter anymore if Shep thought they may be real agents, Shep didn't give a fuck if they were as far as meth went, it was apparent that if Shep had meth he was going to do it. The scare tactics had run him all the way up to South Carolina, so in a sense the tactics had served the purpose, Shep was not doing meth.

Shep was in the darkness of his room in the bed whispering, It was easier that way, because if he could and didn't, the Recluses kept stabbing him with the same knife till he protected himself, so moving on to the next subject was easier. The light from the hallway came creeping from under the bedroom door. For some reason it had been cut off the floor leaving a noticeable, unusual gap. The more his eyes adjusted to the dark the more it became noticeable. It lit a path that narrowed, ending up in the opened closet on the opposite side of the room. Shep's imagination was being pulled in the closet by something hanging, the super large buttons maybe from a coat, The wrinkles of a dress with sequins on it, all kinds of things loosely hanging side by side in that dim light, was staring back at Shep with two large almond shaped eyes, framed on one side by a egg shaped face, to dark to see the other side, it's long skinny arm hung by the side of a narrow body, it was an alien alright, straight from X-Files. He knew it was just an illusion.

The Recluses had to keep a chain on it, Shep had only thought about it. The conversation was some where else so he did not mention it out loud,, just yet.

Scooter saw the opportunity, he figured unleashing an alien would be just as well as a beast. He made his way over to the mic on the table.

Shep and Scooter's minds were in the closet with the alien. Scooter cut the chain roaring over Dumbass. "SHEP THERE AIN'T NO GOD DAMN ALIEN IN THAT FUCKING CLOSET!!!

Shep raised up to sitting position whispering loudly. "Your reading my mind?" The chain had been cut he was over whelmed. The feeling of disappointment, he wanted to be a human bug. If he was not a human bug how could he prove it and save the world.

Shep instantly saw the burden of the endless conversation, nothing held back. His every thought a opportunity for a feeding frenzy, like sharks. He learned from experience they could and would take any thing no matter how good and twist it into bullshit. Shep was wise in not getting twisted with it but the sheer negativity was not his natural style. Those thoughts/feelings came instantaneously as he started to plan.

Scooter reassured Shep as he looked around the table at the others with stun looks on their face. "Yea, Shep, we damn show are. We have been reading your mind for months, The Machine, as we call it back in the mountain has been learning you better and better, I am as blown away as you are by this shit Shep and believe me I thought I had seen it all, till I worked with some others to build The Machine."

Shep was trying to make sense of it all and plan his survival. He figured it could be some level of quantum mechanics that was only known by few or maybe it was simple as hooked on phonics. The sounds of the English language each being a group of neurons in the brain holding a charge of electrons in some chemical waiting to be released by the influence of other releases all over the nerves system highways, billions of them neurons in a constant complicated but simple for that is all it is chemical reactions fed by the food we eat the air we breath and influenced by our senses. It's that flow of electrons that is Phonics that can be turned to electromagnetic force. If conducted through the right material , no matter how small. He announced in a whisper. "That brings me back to nanobugs."

The plan of all this was, even knowing that the mind reading put this adventure in the realm of skitzo, he had to survive it, and what better way to do that than have a reason that was larger than life to keep him going. Seeing that the world was still faced with the threat of nanobugs, not ones that could read minds, that's just crazy, but the powder that could be put in ones food or drink and combine with the power source, the nervous system, and not only pick up the vibrations of sounds around them and from them, it also could turn the nerves of their ears into speakers, being vibrated with crystals. He knew that some technology like nanobugs would be possible soon, if not already. Shep was going to keep living the life of a human bug, just in case. Just in case, Hell I reckon in case there is mind reading technology and aliens on earth and the moon is made of cheese and we all was made by the magic of a powerful wizard.

Scooter liked the way this was heading he didn't care much for the world being infested with nanobugs. He gave Shep some words of encouragement. "Man, if I was not standing here talking to your thought's I would not, in a million years believe that we created this technology, it still seems impossible and I had a hand in making it. Just keep doing what you planned to do. I kind of feel like Einstein after he helped make the nuclear bomb, it's bitter, sweet. I had to see if it could be done now I wish it couldn't have. This will continue as was 24/7 every second, it's for your own good, if you live through it. 20% what happens to you 80% what you do about it. What are you going to do about it man? Give him hell men."

With that, Scooter left and Shep got his first night of what was his life from now until, was the question. If it was just his own mind gone haywire as he truly believed now, then if he made it to 100 it would be a miserable life at this rate. Every thought invited some hell along with it. His natural keep a positive outlook being challenged till his death. Having to fall asleep in the middle of conversation that never ended. Imposable to ever ignore. When something is said we are capable of not responding, but the thought of is unstoppable. He got off to a good start as the Recluses stomped on his brain. He let his nature take over and rolled with the punches. He thought "Well, at least I am off work from Wal-Mart tonight, I would have hated to start this and put shit on a shelf."

Dumbass hollered. "SHEP YOU WILL QUIT THAT JOB, YOU WILL NOT SURVIVE US!"

A MIB, "Shep I ain't worried about that. I want to know what about all this money I got bet on your timely demise, I think this knew revelation is a game changer."

MIB responds, "All bets are final that's what I say nothing has changed in the game because, it's a game of life and life is like a box of chocolates……."…………………………….......................on an on an on an on they never shut up. Shep stopped whispering.

Chapter 27

The morning after the first all night of snow ball headed for hell thought conversation, Shep found himself jogging the trail. Staying in the bed in endless conversation, was easy to do because of the lack of sleep, but sleep was not possible, and that only lead to depression. Not from the topics, he could handle the bad raps. The feeling of now knowing more than ever that this was his haywire brain not the meth, based on the fact that the longer he went with out meth the worst they got. Was this his life till death?

Pushing himself to the limit was the rush of sprinting the last mile of the trail. The obstacles and scenery of the trail took his mind off the distance. The sound of his on foot steps being plaid back to him out of step with a bat in it's hand didn't hurt his speed.

His thinking was on planning the human bug war, first set up his defense, in case the CIA wanted to make him disappear. It didn't matter if he was a human bug or not, just if he was right about their existence.

Hearing Shep think about the end of the woods the foot steps behind him fell back with threats carrying a slight echo sound, just like they came from the woods. "Next time Shep your ass is ours!" "Shep I lost you way back!" "Shep that's because he's a fat ass!"

Then the voices that were still talking to him as though they sat on his shoulder commented on the pond Shep was walking around. "Swim for it Shep."

Shep had one word for that. "Snakes."

"You pussy." "Shep I'm with you on that, snakes." Shep somebody just walked in. Tell Shep what we got here man." "Shep I just got back from the store and I don't have this guy the kind of Mountain Dew he wanted. They did not have it, so he got regular, but I got the rest of the shit. What have I missed?"

Shep said out loud "I got chased by spiders, big ones." He thought the rest to the Bluetooth's.

It was Sunday he made his way down the driveway with his hands on top of his head, catching his breath. Seven year old Katelyn, straight brown hair dancing to her excited walk, blue eyes looking for adventure, met him. She had a empty peanut butter jar in one hand, the lid in the other.

Shep took notice. "What's up with the jar lil' lady?"

She showed the emptiness of the jar. "I'm chasing butterflies."

Making their way down the driveway the voices had jokes. "Shep I see you in a loony bin gown chasing butterflies with a butterfly net."

Yellow butterflies floated and fluttered from reed to flower in crazy number. She would chase them but not too far from her knew friend. Far from the catching, the chase lead around to the dock where Shep used a fish scooping net to swipe a big one and put it in her jar. She slapped the lid down and boasted of the catch.

He looked at the big yellow wings flapping violently. "Ya' know what baby, if you let it go you get to make a wish." His brilliant plan to free the beautiful creature and free some greed from Katelyn's heart.

"What can I wish for?"

"I reckon anything."

Mind-you the Agents still yelling from across the pond and on his shoulder one even gargling water as he spoke.

Katelyn opened the jar and the butterfly joined it's kind. Shep asked her what she wished for. She grinned. "I wished that all the butterflies in the world was mine."

Shep stood on the dock feeing like a sucker. His lesson in greed had backfired. He smiled, "I hope I stand a better chance at saving the world from nanobugs."

It made no sense to her. "What?"

"One day you'll find out with the rest of the world."

The voices, "Your a stupid son of a bitch Shep!" "Shep you can not save the world with plans like that."...........................

Her mama called to her from the house and she skipped away. Shep thought he had under estimated his opponent.

A Recluse jumped on him. "Shep so that's the way you see it, that little girl is your opponent?"

"No, my opponent was greed, man, greed."

Chapter 28

Having anything like rest had been pushed out of Shep's reach. Finding himself waking up after not being asleep, but in constant conversation with voices all the while. The days of mind reading had turned to weeks. Being no win for him in fight he made it point not to argue with them.

At Wal-Mart Shep had to deal with constant conversation with a new level of tolerance. It was not something that he was getting used to and his stock time was showing it. Keeping his patience hard to do. He didn't show it physically, he didn't see it as a physical thing. His mental blood grew to a boil after considerable amount of, "Shep go to the other row.", "No, no Shep it's right there in front of you.", "Shep If you just stop, and listen to me I will lead you in the right direction, take those beans put them over there by the end of the row and I'll be there to get them in a little while."
......................CONSTANT.................

Shep pulled the rod back with a short jerk and reeled in some more line slowly. His thoughts sunk like the lead and plastic minnow, being dragged slowly in a world separate form the world above the surface.

Sue's voice brought him up for air. "Hello, you in to that fishing? I asked you do you need anything from the store?"

Shep turned to see her walking past him up to the waters edge with a bag of stale bread, tossing the bread in pieces to the water causing the ducks from across the pond to come squawking. . He joked, "I didn't know you were into sneaking up on me."

"That hasn't been hard to do lately."

Shep recast and reeled in slowly. The voices in his world cast out one of their own, "Shep don't you bother telling her what your thinking. She is in on it man." "It's true her and Will have been told if Will wants to keep from being investigated he has to forget what he found out about us."

This kind of bullshit was a normal occurrence and Shep didn't let it effect his decision making. He laid it on her. "I got some bad news and good news, the bad news is my human bug theory was shot to hell, on account they started reading my mind a few weeks ago. Now I'm stuck in this perpetual insanity of a conversation with the same Brown Recluses that came here with me. The good news is I just told you about it, saving you weeks of worry."

She looked like she didn't know what to say. "What the Fuck?"

"It all started with this alien in the closet." He got big blue bug eyes wide looking back at him in the bright sun of the day. He stopped reeling the line in and continued before she lost it. "Let me explain, not a real alien it was just ………." he gave her the 45 second version.

She questioned. "Do we need to get you a shrink?"

"If you know one that will prescribe me some Benzedrine."

"I'll see if Will can get you something to help you sleep." She was walking to the car.

Shep cast out. "No Benzedrine is speed, I lay in the bed enough, I need an antidepressant and that's the best I know."

She disagreed with his remedy. "That's what started all this."

Shep felt a nibble on the line and jerked back hard. The Recluses hearing him think. "Got one." they stopped yelling whatever they had been, "…good fucking try Shep, but no speed for you!" "Shep you stupid son of…………….." to "get him Shep get him…." "Damn her, get that fish, man……………." Shep explained to Sue as she opened the car door. "And that's what is going to finish it, but I'll take a six pack of Bud in the bottle and a pack of smokes now. I don't like drunk, it would be nice though to chill and sip one down, and unwind a little."

She said out the car window loudly "See you don't know what you want to do!"

Boy, this gave them voices something to rag him about and they did not miss the opportunity. Shep was comfortable with his statement, Sue had left the driveway by then. "I'm just like anybody else, some times they want this and some times they want that."

About 45 minutes later, Will came pulling up in his black Honda Accord. On his way in the house he shouted down to Shep. "You had best get some rest you will be going to work tonight."

The voices "…..Daddy Will said…………." "Shep this is Prep, look I had to take my 3 year old daughter to the ER last night, bad ear ache, and I was hoping you would go lay down so these loud ass mutherfuckers might calm down a little, and I could take a nap, so take your ass to bed like daddy Will said."

Shep was hooking the hook to the pole and walking up toward the house. "A nap sounds good, If you can keep them quiet……."

"FAT CHANCE ON THAT !!!!…….."

Sue pulled in the drive with Buddy the 10 ten year old beanpole, Jessica 12 looked like her mama spit her out and Katelyn came piling out the car. Sue motioned Shep to the back seat floor board where he found a six pack of bottle Budweiser and a pack of Marlboro. He thanked her and asked the children how there day went. The beer went in the frig.

On the way to work that night Sue expressed her and Will's concern of him getting on some meds to get control over the voices. Shep remembering the experience of the meds at the mental hospital declined. "I really don't think it will help. I think I'm just going to have to deal with them. I know you can't grasp it, because your not hearing it, but it's like they are so real they are going to do what they want to do." He explained his human bug war plan, emphasizing he was going on the shadow of a possibility that human bugs do or will exist and he was going to prepare the world for it. After that she was a little more sure he needed to get some help.

It was a long night at work for him and the next morning he relaxed with a beer on the porch over looking the lake, his mind below the surface of the world. One of the agent's kept saying over and over. "Shep what about the….?(he would stop and wait on Shep to think response, then the agent would disagree. "No, no, no Shep. What about the…..?" It had become a regular thing they would do with different question's every so often. It was easy for them to do that because they just recorded the question and then put it on repeat using the computer. Other agent's would continue with, whatever, at the same time.

Shep tried to let it roll off him like water off them ducks on the pond.

Chapter 29

Shep was walking up and down the isle at Wal-Mart with another can of beans in mid-bullshit.

One of the Recluses sitting at in the cabin at the picnic table, "Shep it sounds like you are.,,,,,,,,,," He was making Shep finish the sentence and every thought Shep gave was the wrong answer. The two being in conversation on another topic. The agent had not bothered hitting the repeat button.

Shep kept uncontrollably thinking an answer, but immediately returned to the topic. ",,,lost. I don't know why I bother telling y'all what you already know. All your voices are on the voice masking program y'all have on the computer. I picture one of y'all at the mic…" he was interrupted.

The agent finished Shep's sentence. "…and the other three working this shift are sitting on their asses on the couches, and I'm having a picnic, at this table and it sounds like you are.,,,,,"

Shep went on ",,,very smart. Now if you talk for thirty minutes or so and while switching your voice to other voices it would sound like y'all are all talking."

One of the agents on the couch spoke up. "Sometimes we all do talk, but I am watching ESPN news with this ear bud in my ear so I can hear the TV and you can't, and I got this Bluetooth in my other ear so I hear you thinking, and commercial just went off so later Shep."

Agent at the table repeated. "Shep it sounds like you are.,,,,,"

Shep finished ",,,picturing y'all as real people when y'all ain't."

Another voice joined in from the couch. "I don't know Shep I feel pretty damn real sitting on this couch surfing the web on this laptop."

It was all day endless

Another week at Wal-Mart and Shep was canned. He could not get the shit on the shelf fast enough. This got Will's attention. He called Shep and Sue to the kitchen table. "Sue tells me that you are having a lot more trouble with the voices than you previously did."

The voices all into it. "…………………..Bitch slap that motherfucker Shep………..."

Shep understood Will's concern. "Yea, now its turned into an endless non stop conversation with them on a whole nother' level, due to them reading my mind now, they just started doing that recently. It is impossible to ignore something like that cause it is impossible not to think a response to every thing they say and what they say I hear in my ears like I hear you talking."

Will had a questionable look on his face. "So what are they saying right now?"

"One of them was just saying that I will never get another job in this town. Another one was hollering that he left his popcorn in the microwave too long and that pisses him off. Another one was yelling that it stinks in the cabin now and he thinks I should get off my ass and go find another job. It's endless man they never stop."

Will leaned way back from the table and looked at Sue like he had bit off mare than he cared to chew. "Sue has found a private mental hospital just down the road in Pinehurst. We think you need to consider going to get some help."

Shep considered it as a place he would be stuck with very little environmental input, and zombied out on some antipsychotic meds that didn't knock a dent in the voices He was already in the bed a lot engulfed in the conversation. He was tired mentally, no matter how positive he kept his mind it was a cover up of the meltdown. But he had the option of getting some fresh air and going for a run, fishing, talking with the kids, it's what kept him alive. "I tell you what, I'd feel better if I just gave it another shot, find another job and learn to deal with them I don't see them going away no matter what. If I can get another job and I loose it, then I'll go get help."

Sue and Will looked at each other and Sue shrugged her shoulders, speaking up. "Are you sure? I have been reading about this on the web and they have some good success with the meds they have these days."

Shep stuck to his guns. "I understand your concern, but I have been there tried it and the side effects, even if they did make the voices go away, are just as bad as the voices. I just need to get another job."

The Recluses kept. "Shep it sounds like you are.,,,,,,,,,, " "Shep go to the nut house we will shut the fuck up if you go, we swear." "Shep I don't give a fuck where you go I am going to kill you before Christmas and get my money I got put on your head."…………………..

Will and Sue had no choice but to let Shep give it another try. Sue took him on another job search the next day and he put a few in online.

Four night's later Shep was inhaling the cold night air, walking into Kroger where Sue had let him out as the new stock boy. The atta'-boys came from the shift of Recluses. Shep put his hands in the pockets of his leather coat Sue had packed for him, when she went by his mom's, before picking him up at the loony bin. He found a surprise two grams of long lost meth. He got so excited he cut a lil' jig right there on Kroger's dance floor. The one just inside the entrance door.

The Recluses stole his thoughts and started stomping on them. "…OH! HELL! NO! SHEP!……….." You can imagine what a bunch of Recluses said, I'll spare you the details.

Shep had his remedy, straight to the tin foil isle he went, no one was around so he helped himself to a good piece of it, folded it up, put it in his pocket and was in the bathroom stall running his lighter under it, before you could say "Don't do it.". Inhaling the smoke freestyle, no straw, right off the foil. He held the smoke in his lungs as long as he could stand it and repeated it several times. He dipped his finger in the bag, retrieving a small mound and stuck it up his nose with a strong snort. He composed his self and off to find the supervisor to get his vest and name tag for another night of putting shit on a shelf at a new place. Them Recluses cussing him for all he was worth and then some.

It was getting close to quitting time the sun was on the rise. He was putting some cereal on the shelf when a mom with her 12 year old, blue eyed, long blond hair, with the face of what he would imagine an angel would have, crossed his path. Shep could not help thinking how pretty she was and how when she got older she would be a heart breaker.

The agents had changed shifts being four knew/old voices. They already being in a frenzy about the meth Shep had in his pocket saw it as an opportunity to rag Shep with unfounded criticism. "It looks like we got a child molester on our hands men." "I heard it too." "Shep you sorry piece of shit, I got a good mind to send some DEA there now and lock you up." "Shep you better go flush it they on the way you child molester."

Shep went to explaining. "No it was nothing like that I would not touch her. If you saw her you couldn't help noticing her beauty."

"See Shep you was looking at that little girls booty."

Shep continued to try and explain for a minute, realizing that it didn't matter what he said they was not going to let up. He quit explaining the best he could and tried to change the subject, with little success. At that time he had no intention's of flushing the meth.

At home he did more meth and stayed away from everybody, he felt like they would be able to tell. The Recluses agreed with him. Eight hours passed and a knew shift came on and Tiffina was in his ear on this shift.

She told him, She felt what they was doing, going on and on about child molester's was under handed. Then backed up the, "If you flush it we will stop talking." She added. "For good."

Shep did some more and made it through another night at work. The next morning, at home, he was, for some foolish reason, entertaining the idea of flushing the last gram down the toilet. He tried to fake it, but the Bluetooth told on him. They had brain washed him by repeating over and over that they would shut the fuck up."

Sterling's voice showed up. "Look my friend, this was a test. When your mama was packing your stuff she found that meth and called me wanting to know what to do with it. I came over and hid it in your jacket pocket and I promised my self that if you found it and flushed it I would call it quits and get out of your head."

Shep corrected him. "Ears"

"Your ears. I am a man of my word. Just let the rest of that shit go and we will let you go, I swear."

Shep didn't even believe they were real people, he just acted like it because it helped him deal with it. With that he was thinking, maybe they was real enough to make a deal and up hold it. What if he did not flush it and it was his way out. All he had to loose was a gram."

This thinking got him a lot of, "Shep you heard it from the man himself, he had a plan and he is going to stick to it." "Shep I don't mind loosing my money, I bet you would kill yourself in two years or less. If we leave you alone, it go's to the men that bet we would end up leaving you alone." "Shep lets end this I am sick of going back and forth to Virginia every week."

Shep stood in the bathroom that evening, did him one more line and took a big puff off the foil, then dropped the almost full gram down the toilet. In the swirl of the flush the voices went silent. Shep took notice. The water started filling the tank. At the same time the sound in his ears cranked up to full volume. "YOU STUPID SON OF A BITCH!" YEA, SHEP THAT WAS THE STUPIDEST THING I EVER SEEN ANY BODY DO!" ……………………. That's exactly how Shep felt too. It was another long night of putting shit on a shelf. They did stop ragging him about thinking that girl was pretty. It had dwindled to nothing, like they just got tired of talking about such a subject.

Chapter 30

Kroger did not last long, maybe stocking just was not Shep's thing. He had made a deal. He was laying, fully clothed, mid-day, hands behind his head propped on a pillow, on a single mattress bed in a room that looked like a mid cost motel room.

The shrink was looking like she was trying to win a Jody Foster look-a-like contest. Shep didn't mind, hell there's been a President of the United States shot to get Jody's attention. She sat in a chair at the end of his bed. "I'm Doctor, Holliday. I need to ask you a few questions, do you feel up to it.?"

"You have my attention, fire away."

"How long have you been hearing voices?"

Shep was being bombarded by the voices, saying all kinda' stuff" He told her how they started, giving her the quick nano version. He let her know he knew that his skitzo may have imitated life, painting a picture with the colors of what was going on at the time. He added that the nanobug thing seemed so real, it was not hard to believe they were real agents, but, it was hard to believe they were not real, so he was believing the hard to believe.

She admitted that the story was the most persuasive conspiracy skitzo, "Why my voices are real" story she had heard so far. In fact most who are experiencing the voices and are die hard set on the Fed's or whoever is talking to them think they had been picked for no reason at all. She stressed she was not saying she in anyway believed he could possibly be a human bug. She put him on some skitzo meds and slipped in a contrary comment. "Although in your case this may not help at all."

He would be there a few weeks for observation. At dinner that night he sat at fold out tables and chairs. The dinning area and TV room is one big room with couches, coffee tables, pic's hang on the walls. His co-patients sat with him at the tables. Two stood out a small, grey haired woman of maybe 85. She sat beside him and he introduced himself. She did the same.

 Shep then did what he normally did. "I'm from Dry Branch, Georgia."

She was looking at him with goo, goo eyes and a grin. She leaned closer to him and bald up one of her little fist. "Well here's to looking at you kid." then she very lightly south pawed him on the chin.

Shep was thinking that it was one of them things he would never forget. The Recluses, stunned. "Don't let that shit go to your head Shep." "Shep I'm jealous, I really am."………………

Shep liked them old movies with Bogart, Grant, Audrey and Katherine Hepburn, etc. With his very small tea glass, he toasted in her direction. "Right back at ya' doll face."

Across from him sat a twenty-ish girl with shoulder length black hair a slightly pointed nose and chin, and high cheek bones. Her sky blue eyes held his attention and she knew it. Her attention had fell into him.

The Recluses constantly trying to shoot him down in flames.

After dinner, Shep was at the desk in his room drawing with some gel pens. He liked to make randomly curving lines in blind format, then look at it from all perspectives till he saw, with some connection between them, they could form a picture of his fantasies. Then he colored it in with varieties of gel pens.

His peripheral vision noticed the young girl, thin but perky, standing in the hall looking in. He said. "Hey"

She came in his room. " I'm Amanda."

"I'm Shep, from Dry Branch, Georgia. It's in the middle of Georgia."

"I'm from here in Pinehurst."

Shep put down his gel pen and gave her his attention. "I ain't crazy I just got a few voices in my ear, but it all makes perfect sense to me. They do get on my nerves though. What are you here for?"

Speaking of the devil, they was going crazy trying to make him feel some sort of way.

She sat on the end of his bed. "I am bipolar."

The Recluses. "Great Shep you two nuts will have a lot to talk about."

He picked up his unfinished drawing. "I never understood how people couldn't have some control over their feelings till these voices started in my ears and I have no control over them at all, I guess that's how you feel about your feelings."

She smiled "That's what it's like. What are you drawing?"

He explained the method to the madness of his art work. She told of things she liked to do. He gave a very brief description of his nanobug theory. She liked it. Shep sat on the bed beside her close but not too close. They gazed in each others eyes a lot and had a few laughs. He was actually in two and three conversations at one time. She seemed to be on the better end of bipolar. He was enjoying himself more than he had since before he was locked up in the first nut house. She surprised him with how they were going to treat her mental state.

Shep showed his surprise. "Electroshock therapy, I did not know they still did that."

"Yea" She explained the procedure.

Shep wondered if it would fry his nanobugs. He knew it would take more than a 120 volt light socket he had done tried that.

A little over an hour they sat and talked. It felt right when they leaned into each other and kissed.

She said she was turning in for the night and stood to leave holding his hand till she was out of reach looking back at Shep with the same look he had on her, like they wanted to go further.

`   Shep asked if they check the rooms at night.

"No the lady just sits down on the other end of the hall and watches TV and they come around early in the morning to check blood pressure and all."

"What if I come to your window? It's a Melissa Etheridge song, Come to my window, climb inside, wait by the light of the moon"

"Never heard it"

"That's a shame. So shall I?"

"I guess, yea."

That night they went slow and soft. He held her till they knew their time was up. THEM DAMN VOICES TRIED TO RUIN EVERYTHING but he didn't mention them to her. It would have been more pleasant with out them but all things considered one of the most remarkable nights of his life.

The next day they had breakfast together and she was took off to electroshock treatment. It was not her first time and didn't seem odd to her but it was Shep's first time and it was fucking crazy to him. He didn't show it, not wanting her take it the wrong way. He had always been pretty good at view switching. Not that everybody would agree with that, say like his ex-wife, Tiffany. He has gotten better at it with age.

Amanda was back before lunch. To Shep's unexpected surprise her mom and dad and little sister had came back from over at the main hospital with her. They packed her stuff to take her leave. Shep kept his distance, they made eye contact a few times and her smile was enough to let him know it was OK.

A few days later the Shrink came back to see him. She said she had looked over his medical records and noticed there had been no MRI done to see if he may have a brain tumor. Apparently they can cause voices. She asked if he could pay and that was a negative.

She said she would send the paper work to get it done with government assistance. It would be a week or two. She had him an appointment for a CAT scan the next day and if it showed something then it would be an emergency then he would go to the more detailed picture of the MRI immediately. If the ex-rays of the CAT scan showed nothing then he would have to wait for the MRI that would turn some of the elements in his body into little radio stations.

Shep asked her in a joking manner, "If I am a human bug that MRI may rip my nervous system apart. So, shouldn't I be checked for nanobugs first?"

She laught. "Lets just get through this CAT scan first."

Three days later the CAT scan had shown nothing to be alarmed about. Dr. Holliday was in her office she had started the process of funds for Shep's MRI earlier that morning and it sat on a mail rack to go out the next day. Two black suites, white men, looked middle aged, clean cut, and athletic, came in her door and flashed some government issued credentials.

One of them spoke with out greetings. "Dr. Holliday, this is a matter of national security. It would be in everybody's best interest if Shep did not have that MRI."

She was not intimidated. Rather she just did not see herself taking on something like this, her life was fairly simple and she liked it that way. They wasn't going to nano-bug her if she could help it. She reached over in her mail basket and took Shep's out going paper work and dropped it in the trash. "Will that be all?"

The second agent found it sufficient. "Thank you for your co-operation, That will be all." They left.

He had tried the meds but after three days of it he started spitting them out. It was some new better meds, that made him feel twice as looloo as the other ones did. He had spent a vast majority of the time laying on his bed in groundless conversation with the Recluses. TV's not to interesting when you loose your page as though it were a book, except once it was lost there was no finding it. The old lady left to go to the main hospital a week after they had met and never came back. She was not much for company. She knew, very soon she was going to find out what happens when you die, and it scared her. She did not say it. It could be seen in her eyes.

The Recluses had been caring on about Amanda committing suicide and it was all his fought for "Taking advantage of her". Of course they had 24 hours a day to fill, so if it could be imagined it probably got talked about.

All that and Shep could not complain. He felt that night to remember with Amanda was worth it, no matter what Dumbass, Prep, and the others said. Tiffina was cool when she worked. She did say she hated her period and was going to take it out on Shep. Sterling had not talked much at all since the beginning, guess it hit a little to close to home knowing Shep all Shep's life. The rest of them was raising hell when their shift first started but planed out before long spiking periodically till the next shift came in.

Shep was told two weeks after the financial aid was supposed to be applied for that it was not going to cover the MRI. That there was nothing left for him to do but go home. Back to Sue he went and the only change was he was fixing to get a new job......Somewhere.

Chapter 31

Sue and Shep was out job hunting, Shep was telling her how he could handle it what ever came his way. He had to in order to survive, so if he lost the next job he could handle it, on to the next one. "Hey, Sue you just passed the place, dang we got to go a mile just to cross the divider." If Shep only knew how that moment was to sum up his next job.

Shep must have made a good impression. He kept the nano's to him self. The 24 year old owner of the pool & spa service company had took his college fund his parents had saved up for him and went out on his own. He was doing pretty good, having enough accounts to keep him going in winter and Shep was the man. It was not cold, cold but getting cooler.

Shep's parent's always had covered their pool with a way big trampoline mat and then chemicals and filtering, and a lot of it, would bring the green water back to clear. It was just easier and probably cheaper to just keep it clean during the winter. At least that's what the pool service company owner will tell you.

This young man knew what he was doing with 3 service trucks running and he also helped out when needed, Shep just listened and took notes during his training period of six days of riding around with the owner or one of the others, testing water, netting off leaves, adding the correct amount of chemicals. It was easy enough the six days was so Shep would get it down pat and sound like he half ass knew what he was doing if a customer was to go asking. That's why the company had done so well, great customer service had started a chain reaction.

Shep made it through the training period with out telling anybody about the voices. He got keys to a truck, that he left at the office every evening. The first day he drove around in three towns with way too many roads. They had been built nearly on top of one another. It was decided, by him and the Recluses, to be a maze set up by some great lab coat wearing scientists in the sky. The scientist did it just to see if Shep would find the pools, only they kept moving thing around so he was forced in circles. The map he had was just to fuck with his head.

Them spiders in his ears was not helping in the least. "Shep you missed the turn!" Shep did you run that red light, you got to calm down and pay attention!" "Shep you need to get over and turn"

Shep was surprised at how much it was ruffling his feathers, He tried to just tune them out and he did not follow to their directions. But a few hours and he was way behind on the list to do. He could call and ask the boss but he would be calling every 20 minutes the dude liable to think Shep didn't know how to read a map. Shep normally could, so he thought, and that constant, "SHEP SPEED UP,,,,,, SLOW DOWN" pissed him off.

He made it back to the office on time, explaining his dilemma as first day, getting a feel for the roads. He was told it would come to him, just look at the map.

Shep was picked up by Will. He stopped and bought Shep a six pack of Budweiser in the bottle, and Shep didn't even have to ask. He told Will that he was probably going to make employee of the month.

"Really?"

"No not hardly. I don't know who designed the roads here and I wouldn't care to know him."

"You got a map?"

Shep let it go. "Never mind I don't want to talk about it."

Will laughed.

The next day was worst than the second and Shep just laughed, faking laughed but he laughed. Not to the boss, he apologized and told him he was going to get better the next day.

Shep made it his first week of driving and things stayed about the same but barely the lack of sleep was causing confusion and Shep was feeling like he was letting the company down. He wanted to tell them that surly they could find somebody that didn't have a bunch of voices in his ear, that him out there driving kamikaze. But he smiled and said I think I'm getting better at it and the boss told him to hang in there.

Shep made it one more week and through in the towel. It was way to dangerous for him to be driving around in his condition his mind was too exhausted to do the job. It almost made him feel like he had some how let it beat him. He decided that two weeks is more than most would have made it so he gave him a pat on the back.

With the check he got from the pool company he was informed by Will that his debt to Sue's mama was paid close enough for him. Shep wasn't sure if that meant he was going to take care of the little left or just fuck it. He didn't ask either. He just said "I appreciate everything I'll go pack my bags." He felt like if he didn't get some meth-med real quick them voices were going to beat the life right out of him, his own adrenaline spent long ago, he was crashing. Sue took him to Dry Branch.

Chapter 32

Shep was opening the door to that old light blue and white 73' Chevy truck getting some feed back from the agents. "Shep you are homeless." "Shep all you got to do is go to the salvation army that's where people like you go."

He climbed in the truck thinking he hadn't seen Shaky in about a 8-9 months. The trip was a lot longer than the original three day tour he set out on to get some help. If it did any good it may have kept him out of prison. Several of the folks he knew and a few more had been sent to the pin for manufacturing meth. He had found out real quick that Dry Branch was not dry at all. In fact he was geeked up already, Only been home 3 days. Deryl let him crash there but he needed to go soon as possible Shep agreed and had a job the next day. It felt great too. He was in his neck of the woods and felt more "how to act."

A little deeper into Dry Branch from Deryl's he turned in Shaky's driveway, the 50yrd. down hill slope had him patting the break. The double wide trailer surrounded by woods a neighbor just to the left a little ways and one to the right that couldn't be seen. Shaky's newer white Ford truck was there, and a grey Jeep Cherokee that he didn't know.

Knocking on the door he was hearing his scorns for being geeked up and he honestly did not give a shit what they had to say. Although he gave his thoughts to them but he didn't even care what he thought. The door opened and Shaky's, the Toby Keith looker, invited him in.

The trailer looked like a trailer on the inside, it was well kept, the blue carpet still looked knew the furniture was nice it was kept clean. Shaky had sat back in the reclining couch seat and on the other side recliner was what looked to be a 6 ft. young lady maybe about 25, long straight down her back hair that was pulled over her shoulder. Her face was that of a tall girl, her body was not big, it was not skinny it was average.

Shep decided small talk would be odd for him with the big question on his mind. "Good to see you man, been a while." He looked at the girl, "I'm Shep good to meet ya'" Back to Shaky. " I got a job at Metal Concepts, got transportation and need a place to stay, wondering if you would be interested in renting one them rooms back there."

Shaky smiled, "Till you can get on your feet right?"

"Be out of here in no time at all." They knew this would end up being a chapter in their life to remember.

Shaky introduced Sara saying "She lives here too, in my room, with me."

Sara looked at him like he could have done better than that. "God forbid you get it right one time."

They talked for a while. The voices did all the time Shep didn't mention them and neither did Shaky. Shep started on his second beer and Shaky grabbed another. Just past the frig the two stepped out on to the back porch. Shaky had that shakee look. They leaned on the rail fired up cigarettes.

Shaky just wanted to make sure all the cards were on the table. "So how is it going with them voices, I just been told by somebody that you was still hearing them in South Carolina. I mean it's alright as long as you don't go doing some crazy shit end up,,,well,,you know."

"Nothing to worry about. They went from my windows down here to in my ears up there. They quit only listening to my environment, now they listen to my thoughts too, so got me stuck in a perpetual conversation. But that's all they can do is talk. If they tell me to go jump in a fire I got enough since not to jump in a fire till *I* am good and ready."

"Sticks and stones may break my bones but word's will never hurt me, right?"

" Shaky there ain't nothing farther from the truth."

Shaky did that chuckle he dose. "That bad huu?"

Shep patted him on the shoulder and started leaning toward going back in the trailer. "Man it is a long story, I'll have to tell ya' bout it later, you wanna' do a bump."

Shaky had a memory. "Oh yea, hold up, I mean yea but, about that…."

"Hey I got ya' you want ever see nothing but a lil' personal and some to share, and ain't no way I'd cook dope any were around here, I couldn't handle your nervous ass."

"And that girl in there is cool but she don't fuck up like we do. She just a weekend warrior, and let's don't say nothing about them voices till she gets to know you a little better."

"Suit your-self, you got some foil?"

Voices in the bugs ears. "You are fucking up Shep, we can't let you do this," "Shep you better believe you going to jail if keep on the path you on. We have a commitment to up hold the law and I take it very serious." "Shep this is Prep man, I am going to remind you of the words Sterling said, If y'all don't stop doing what you doing y'all going down like dick sucking clowns."

Passing it to Shaky, Shep exhaled the air left in his lungs , thinking. "We could bring up the point we been over a million times. You, crossed the line when y'all bugged me, and come to think of it I ain't going to have any win chasing that rabbit so let's do this…" Shaky handed him the Foil back and asked him if he made it.

"Naw somebody gave it to me, welcome home present" He finished his thinking "….Let's do this. Since we all got so much in this lets just keep on going and see how this play's out. I got to save the world from nanobuggers like yourself so be a good sport give me a chance to prove it. If Shaky new what I was sitting here thinking to y'all he would,,,, hell he would dig it ."

Shep went to explaining and Shaky just smiled with a damn look on his face. Then started laughing, "Hey man, check this out, how long you think it's going to take you to get up on them feet?"

Shep laid awake in his new room that night knowing his first day at work putting on metal roofs was going to be a long one. He had to rest his bones as much as he could and deal with the brain drain. Them voices was carrying on bout some shit here and some shit there.

A different voice joined in, nothing knew they had used the voice masking to do Donald Duck Mickey Mouse and a few more, but this was Scooter's voice the scientist that had came from the mountain, inside it.

Scooter had been sitting at the table for forty five minutes, typing and moving files around the screen, He was listening to an agent switch his voice around and talking about a few things till Shep turned it all into something different. The agent would look at his watch every so often.

Two other agents were sitting on the sitting on the couches. One was whittling on a log on the porch, said he was turning it into a bear, he would take the mic out to the porch and talk to Shep while he whittled. He kept Shep informed of his progress. As big as he said the log was, and claimed he had a regular old pocket knife, only working one or two days a week, Shep didn't think he would have time to finish it. The Recluse told Shep he had more faith in him than that.

(I told ya' that to tell you this.) Scooter, at the table, told Shep, and all the rest in ear shot, cause they got quite when he talked, He said, "Man I got a mojo for ya' doebroe, This thing is called a copy-catter and that's what this is, or should say what you are, an experiment of technology and just how far humans will go to fuck something up. This computer is called the copy-catter, the rest of this computer is in the mountain. We are all going to take a break from you and see if this thing will take our place well enough for you to keep on talking to it like it is us."

Shep was always thinking right over what they talked about, that's just how things worked, Shep whispered in the darkness of his new room. "And it don't matter that you told me." He thought the rest. "cause if they sound real enough I won't know if this is a skit y'all came up with in the boredom of the cabin or the real thing so I will be compelled to treat them the same."

The men at the cabin had no idea this was happening till Scooter told Shep. It dawned on one of them that they would be sent to other things, and really not being many top secret jobs that allowed them to work 1 or 2 days, a week and get full pay. He said. "Damn it Shep now I will probably go back to that office five days a week searching on a computer for some fucking fucked up code. It paid good so I dealt with it but I done got spoiled, Shep I ain't leaving."

Shep took it at face value, but had that perception of maybe it was a way to make the transition. Like he was supposed to think the computer and real people would be talking so he had the extra task now of figuring the real from the computer all the time.

Scooter stopped Shep's train of thought. "SHEP I can't get that out your head now, it is a possibility and I can't erase those, you just will never know. It is just the computer, I swear, I am only telling you cause I feel like you are my human bug and I can tell you what ever I want. Talk to you later Shep." He pushed the enter button on the computer and they all but the whittler left. There had to be a security guard for all the equipment and just incase the computer broke he could pick up a mic.

Shep never missed a beat. That enter button Scooter pressed, put Scooter's voice in Shep's ear saying "Shep never mind we ain't going anywhere." The computer went and found the recorded sentences of the agents between then and the time Scooter showed up with the copycatted. It found several matches to, "never mind we ain't going anywhere" It pulled some other similar ones and played them back to Shep by this time his mind was thinking a similar or exact phrase and the computer went and found that. It worked, it was faster than Shep could think so he just kept on doing what he had been doing, trying to keep up with the voices, unwillingly. It even turned the voices into shift work like the same old routine.

Shep was thinking "If the copy-catter was real and just assuming the Recluses are real, it must be like, them computers he saw on TV that trade stocks with no human persuasion. The computers adjust the sell and purchase of stock based on the performance of a bunch of other related stocks. Say if the price of Nike Shoe goes up a half a cent due to the glue that holds them together going up cause a ingredient went up witch also is used to make Copper Tone tanning oil then the computer figures this up in billionths of a second and adjusts accordingly, there is the consumer and the producers that influence the market but that computer don't know that it's just turning switches of and on in a pattern influenced by that of another. I'm just saying if it can do that I expect I could talk to a copy-catter, I guess I am like the hundred million dollar man now hooked into that computer, I'll go pawn my brain."

The copy-catter did what it was programmed to do during Shep's long thought out speech. It went and found all kind of related topics and randomly picked one or two and spit them out in the Recluses voice. Every so often it repeated something that was not relevant to the subject at hand just to fit in.

See, Shep's conversations had been going non stop but rarely had more than a few sentences per topic. This gave the copy-catter a vast database of subjects to match the subject on Shep's mind. It returned with sentences from the past and by sentences I mean statements, so that could be several sentences in written form. Being 4 voices per shift it didn't flow in real time, the sporadic nature of the machine was unnoticeable. Anyway that's the low, low on how that shit maybe coulda' worked.

Shep tried to think of subjects that the damn thing couldn't relate to but if he happened to find one it was only for the moment of the thought. It was more of a silly game than any thing. He didn't have much else to do in the back seat of the white truck with the ladders on the ladder rack, tool boxes lined the sides, company logo on the door`, rolling down I-75 south.

It was his first day on the job. Destination: A county school in some not so distant land. He kept the voices to himself. While he was unloading the truck, a near by truck was backing out the drive. The beep…beep…..beep …..beep….. of the safety warning reverse thing was turned into an annoying problem for Shep. Every beep a voice masked syllable in his ear.

"Shep…you….will….nev…..er….ma….ke….it…..for…..get…..a……bout ….this….bull…..shit…." Then the other voices talking regular. "He's right Shep this ain't for you." "Tell that guy you need to go home." Shep knew that all had been said on his first day of work before, maybe it ran a search on his thought of, "Here I go first day." He had said that before.

Then a big industrial fork lift went into reverse and it was talking too. Shep got an uneasy feeling, quickly covering it with positive statements. Some more beeping. He went with the guy he would be working with and got started putting material and tools on an area of the roof they used for staging stuff.

Talking in sounds was nothing knew to him, they had done that from the beginning, refrigerator, the crickets, compressors, window a/c units, the sound of a crowd at a football game on TV. He had found through research that it is a common trait of skitzo's and the like. With voice masking technology it was also a common trait of a human bug. Was it something a copy-catter could do? Shep had doubts. Could it distinguish sounds to mask with. If it did it on the first beep it had to be over laid only a computer would be fast enough to do that. If not then it could have a delayed reaction or it was the same old Recluses talking to him. He thought "Boy I sure put a lot of thought into my brain gone haywire."

The next beeps came and the next and the next, with that he ruled out the first beep it was always the second or third, so maybe no copy-catter.

It was another hell of a first day on the job. The guy he was working with pointed out, "You don't say much do you?"

"Sometimes, I guess today just ain't my day,"

The voices had a lot to say. They talked in the drills in the jack hammers used by other companies, in the firing of nail guns, and the most worst was the constant beeps of something always backing up.

He made it and kinda' enjoyed the first day as far as the crew he worked with and the work he was doing. On the way home in the back of the truck he got a welcomed suprize. Shift change for the Recluses, and Tiffina was in the mix. Computer/copy-catter or not he loved to hear her voice. They all said their hellos.

Tiffina sat on a couch removing her finger nail polish She listened for a while saying little, the copy-catter being a recurring subject. She took a deep breath. "Shep, we have been briefed on this copy-catter stuff and the more I listen the more I don't feel like listening to you go on and on about it all night so I am going to unplug the idea from your fucked up head."

The Recluse at the table butted in. "Hold up there, now we need to talk about this."

Tiffina continued. "Shep, I was thinking if you want proof of no copy-catter I will give you something you have never heard before."

Shep was ahead of her. "Actually you already pretty much cleared it up, that is the most I have heard any of y'all say since this thing started with the copy-catter, and it sounded real."

Tiffina snapped. "Quiet! Shep, the timing of this has to be perfect. You know you have never heard me fart into this mic. Right?"

All was quiet in the truck. Shep thought to the Bluetooth. "No not you but they do it all th……."

Tiffina stopped him. "SHEP! Listen." She stood up off the couch and took the near by mic and put it to her ass.

Shep heard a short fart.

The cabin busted into a laugh giving their loud applause, whistles and comments. "And with that went the copy-catter Shep" "Tiffina, I think they fake it with their mouth." "Shep dose that clear it up for you…" In the mean time Tiffina was bowing, saying, "Thank you, thank you, thank you."

I/Shep told this copy-catter story from the beginning, with the delivery of the box on Scooters arrival and told it as if it had been installed because it shows how I had pictured it all going down as it was being projected to me by the agent's.

Time rolled on a few weeks. He had his meth-med in hand most of the time. Home life at Shaky's produced no complaints. On work nights they chilled and watched TV. Shaky liked Discovery and History channels. Normally Shep would have a hard time paying attention to it, but Shaky like to talk about it, or something it reminded him of, so a good discussion of a mechanical, scientific, or natural kind kept Shep in the room.

On week ends they kicked up a little dust, few folks might show up, throw some stuff on the grill drank a few beers, chase the dragon, crank up the stereo. Shep enjoyed it, not as much as he did at one time, cause a part of him was in the cabin with the Recluses.

He was holding on to his job. Sometimes he got to the shop just in time to catch the truck pulling off to the job site. He never would have made it that far in his gas guzzling truck, taking a half a days pay to get there. It helped keep focused a little telling the agents and beeps and drills, things like. "That is good, what you saying and all but now I am going to put this on the saw table and cut it." They responded with any thing from, "You gonna' fuckit up Shep." to "Shep I don't give a rats ass what you do with it" He said stuff like that 5 thousand times a day.

The rain kept him at home one day and he was alone (you know what I mean) so he took the opportunity to start his Human Bug War by calling some local lawyers offices at random from the phone book. Who ever answered the phone was told. "This is Shep from Dry Branch, and I need you to know that the Feds have developed a a.m. crystal radio that is only a molecule big it is put in food or drink and once in a person billions of them combine with the nervous system making a walking walky-talky- A human bug."

Mixed reaction, from "O dear." to "What you want me to do about it?"

Shep would end with, "I just want you to tell other people about it." and hang up.

Chapter 33

Finishing the job at the school in southern Georgia, Metal Concepts started a job near the Alabama line. Being a good distance away Metal Concepts footed a motel room for four days a week, working 10 hour days.

Shep was having trouble getting ammonia, so cooking was out, he had to pay. He would do most of it before it was time to go back to work Monday morning. The Recluses had got tired of hounding him about it so they just rolled with it. It did make for a long ride at work being with out it.

It worked like an anti-depressant. Knowing he had something to look forward to when he got home kept him going in it's on way. The weather had warmed up and the gnats at work added to his aggravations.

By this time Shep had told the work crew why he seemed so distant. They couldn't believe he would even attempt to hold this job, much less be productive at it. Their hats off to him. They digged the nanobugged story.

One day at lunch Shep excused himself from the restaurant, they were eating at to go next door to a public library. He browsed the science section till a science encyclopedia drew his attention. The 1996 copyright was noticed as he flipped to the N, nanotechnology had a few paragraphs.

His pulse quickened. Crazy enough he had not read any thing about it since the voices had started. It told a short description of it's definition of nanotechnology, Molecules arranged to perform a mechanical function.

He figured in his case the mechanical function would be the vibration of the nano crystals attached through out his nervous system that caused his ear nerves to vibrate and vibrated from the sounds in his environment causing electric current to be turned to nano hertz by the nano bugs and sent to the cabin, or something like that.

He read on. The last paragraph of the four got his heart pounding. In it stated, and this would be as far back as 1996, that, "Nanotechnology was already being combined with DNA." That's all it said about that. Must be a lot of top secret stuff.

Running short on time, needing to get back to the restaurant, he quickly found a old psychology book. Skitzo treatments, read that in the 40's and 50's methamphetamines was prescribed. He could see why it did not take the voices away, hell his was there to stay nano or not, but it did give that boost to go about the day and try to have some part of a normal life.

As luck would have it Dumbass, the stupidest son of a bitch in the world as far as Shep was concerned, was on shift. It seemed to Shep that he took advantage of the fact that Shep could not get his hands on him and he pushed the limits to the max.

Back on the hot, gnat infested, roof, Shep went and Dumbass took the mic. Shep still ain't sure what pushed Dumbass over the line, maybe it was Shep making something out of this nanobug thing one day and him going unknown or maybe he just hated Shep was running wild and free and his life was a drag. Cross the line he did. "SHEP, YOU WILL NEVER AMOUNT TO A FUCKING THING!!!! Shep you left that Katelyn up there with Will and he is ripping her......."

I/Shep can't go into the accusations and the repeated abuse that Dumbass put the many kids in my life through in my mind. I figured it couldn't last, they had never done anything like it. I was wrong. It took a while but what was just Dumbass's voice was joined by the others on shift after Dumbass's voice said. "It's OK y'all, I got the OK."

Shep had to deal with the sick, detailed, bloody descriptions of torture to kids for the rest of that day the sleepless night, the next day on the roof and on the home that evening. He kept what was happening to himself. It was making his blood boil with pure hate and anger toward what ever this was in his ears. He could not live like this even knowing the kids were fine.

Shep got home to Shaky's that night took a shower and said by to everybody in the house, they were going out some where. He sat at the kitchen table, phone in front of him. "Don't do it Shep your going to get locked up." "Shep you a fucking child molester and Mathew is being whipped with a strap as we speak he is being beat Shep you hear me do you hear me."

Shep picked up the phone thinking "If Sterling is in on this he has got to put a stop to it." He did not know Sterling's number but he knew Sonny's,

Sterling's brother. The phone rang and rang, "Hello we are not able to answer the phone, please leave your name and number and we will be in touch." Beeeep.

Shep spoke loud. "This is Shep, Look you tell Sterling if they don't stop talking that shit they talking, I'm going to blow his ass UP!"

It took about 20 minutes for that to sink in. It had no effect on the voices subject except they added to it who Shep was going to jail. He called back and Sonny's wife answered. "This is Shep look I'm sorry I did that but you know what I been going through and the voices have been saying things that are just so bad.."

"Look I understand, but you can't do that, my daughter heard it and she is scared and Sonny's called jones county and they are on the here to listen to it."

"I really ain't going to hurt anybody. I just lost it for a second."

"I'll let them know but you done messed up."

"I know just let them know."

"I will"

"Thank you by"

"By"

Four hours later Shep was in the Jones county jail. That being the destination of the call, being where Sonny lived. He would spend the next 30 day's in the solitary confinement. His ears burning with Tiffany being question by the law, wanting to know if he needed to be put away for life, being a deadly threat to the public. The FBI being on there way to the jail to pic him up and taking him in for questioning, they said he would be doing 20 in the federal pin for terrorist threat on a DEA agent, that they were gearing up to go in and bust everybody Shep had any drug connection with on and on they went. But they said nothing about child abuse, other than stuff like Zack breaking his neck on his dirt bike, now paralyzed from neck down.

What happened was, after Sterling got the news, shortly after Shep's threat was made, he and Scooter came to the cabin relieve Dumbass. Who had not left the cabin in order to give the new shifts coming in an example of what to do, emphasizing he had got the OK on it. He had not got the OK on it, he faked called Martin and lied to the rest of them. Sterling jerked him around a little for "Almost getting him killed." and sent him home, with a "Don't pull that shit again." The talk went back to normal.

Shep's 30 days in the hole WAS FUCKED UP and that is an understatement. Good god they just never shut up. He was let loose on a O.R. bond, that states that they took his word that he would show back up for court on terrorist threat charges. Nobody was more surprised than Shep that they did that.

A charge of terrorist threat on a federal agent was a bit more than Shaky was prepared to deal with spotlighted under his roof. The heat was everybody including the law, knew about Shep and they all figured it all stemmed from meth and they suspected manufacturing .

Shep found himself back at the house where the window voices first appeared. "Trudy I need a place to stay."

With sincerity she declined. "Aw man, you know my parents are my landlords and with all the ummm….."

Shep summed it up. "All the bullshit."

"Yea, but you know my friend Jonny (A stout, shaved head, beaked nosed, thirty year old) ,may let you rent a room from him. He was just by here this morning complaining about being short on his trailer payment."

The good folks at Metal concepts had held Shep's job so this was looking like a good idea. Shep knew Jonny from him stopping by to see Trudy, when he lived there. Jonny had bought a little meth but was mostly about the weed. He lived down in Dry Branch. Shep gave him a call.

Chapter 34

"I appreciate this man. Here's ya' first months rent." Shep and Jonny stood behind the light blue single wide trailer. A few tall pines in a small back yard then thick brush on out. The long gravel driveway put the trailer a good 75 yards off the road. Then it curved behind the trailer where they stood. The front yard was dotted with small neglected shrubs. On the driveway side, the property was separated from the next with a row of dense trees and as well on the far end of the trailer. A 6x6 unused rickety front porch with rotting hand rails a few feet off the ground led to the front door.

Jonny reached out to shake hands. "No problem, I'm glad you came along. I've been sweating the bills. We're short on work at the machine shop. Just a slow two months. We got some big jobs coming up though, so things should pick up."

Shep lit a cigarette. "Hey yaw' want to' hit some foil?"

"You got some?"

Sheep laughed. "I try to keep it but don't worry I isn't going to be dealing or cooking around here."

They chased the dragon in the basics furnished living room. Sheep had the small bed room at the driveway end of the trailer and Jonny's was on the far end. Shep explained he didn't know how much longer the school job near Alabama would last and that he would be gone for days a week. He explained his incarceration and charges as a misunderstanding, like a joke that had gotten taken the wrong way.

Trudy had filled Jonny in on the Brown Recluses way back when. Shep didn't suppose Jonny was ready for the all out human bug experience and left it at, "I hear voices some times, nothing to worry about."

The next month went smooth all thing s considered. Shep made it to work. Rolling with the punches day after day they gave him hell non stop. Laying in the motel room all night listening to the constant dilemmas lies of constant dilemmas back home. On the roof they came at him like the gnats. Mixing voices with the Beeps and surrounding sounds.

It was a Saturday night he was in his small room back in Dry Branch in his shorts laying on the bed. The Recluses had started playing imaginary games at his window again, entertaining them selves.

Prep was at the mic and Shep listened as the illusion of them actually being on the four wheelers riding in the dark night, just out of view if Shep was to peek out the window in his room looking on to the driveway. To his right he could see the start of the back yard and if he looked as far as he could to the left, he just could see the driveway spill onto the road.

Shep played the silly game by thinking along with the scenarios, helping them build crazy houses of cards. The four wheelers disappeared. Prep sped them off, telling Shep they had something special for him. Prep was not sure what he was winging this whole thing with the help of his agent buddies. Some agents were talking just out side his window in Preps absence as if Shep could not hear them and it was such a whisper Shep sat on the floor by the window and raised the blinds enough to see out. They heard his thinking and adjusted the volume up a tad to give him the full effect. . "He should have flushed it." "I know, we been at him all night and we told him it was coming to this." "Yea I hate it but he asked for it………."

The crickets could be heard speaking their mind, long syllables and short words. After an hour it was getting near dawn, he had tried to return to the bed several times but the pulled him back to the window. "I'm so skitzo."

It was getting close to the morning twilight and Prep returned as a voice in his ear, "We will be there in just a minute." Just keeping Shep in the game. The Bluetooth of Shep's thoughts gave him a plan just at that moment. Shep was thinking of the sound of mud tiers winning to a slow. It fit perfect.

What Shep heard was the substitute paper man in a jeep slowing to put the paper in the neighbors paper box. What he saw was nothing but tail lights stop then start backing up, he had passed the box. Prep was in his ear saying "Shep we got to unload this." As the voices just out his window played into it. "Finally their here lets get up there and help." Prep picked one end of the picnic table a half inch off the cabin floor "Get the tail gait" and dropped it." Shep heard a tailgate fall. Prep dragged a fork across the table. "Dam I didn't know a pine casket could be so heavy, you got that side." "I got it, go" The jeep pulled off as Prep dropped the table again.

The reality of it all brought the shadow men out. The grey of the gravel driveway made an excellent backdrop. The very light sound of the pine box crept closer as it was drug closer to the mic and Shep. In his ear talking quietly. "Hold on let me fix my mic" "Shep we told you to flush that shit, and we decided the other day at a pow-wow that we hade to take a more drastic approach to get it in your head that we ain't fucking around."

The box dragged a few feet closer Shep's mind was bucking. "y'all ain't going to get me in that box alive I'll tell y'all that."

"Shep we brought the knock out gas, once we fog the trailer with it you and your buddy there will be out like a light." "Ok you two go ahead and find a place in the duct work under the trailer to flow the fog in, I got snipers one and two with cover, just incase Jonny hears y'all fuck up and comes out shooting." They had heard Shep thinking last week about Jonny having guns and always talking about "I'll shoot that son of a bitch, I will, I'll shoot him." And that could be anybody or thing that he didn't agree with.

Shep could hear one just out side his window around the corner. "Hold on y'all I dropped my Bluetooth over here some where. What has he been thinking?…I got it."

This was sounding so real, and the tail lights, and the shadow men, and even the crickets had stopped talking to listen to all the action. Shep had an over whelming feeling better safe than sorry. He took some books and placed them over the vents in his room, then over the ones in the kitchen and den. Back in his room a voice in his ears "That won't stop us, Shep we will put the tube in this."

The entire time they reminded him. "Shep you should have flushed it." "Shep a few days in this box will get your attention it has got air holes in it, you will be OK." Shep we went through all this trouble you are going in the box."]

He was starring out the window again catching glimpses of the shadow men along the tree line half way up the driveway. He started thinking about leaving, no were to go this early on a Sunday morning but it was ringing in his head. Get in his truck and just drive. The sky started turning grey with light the sun was almost there. He waited and held his breath to hear the slightest sound. He decided that he would leave just a little more light.

Sterling had entered the cabin about ten minutes ago, he would show up at anytime, and was briefed on the skit. One of the agents had bragged me and this guy are snipers. He heard Shep's plan of jumping ship and blocked the plank. "Fuck this shit Shep. I am tired of putting up with your Bull Shit,

Mother FuckER! If you walk out that trailer you're a dead man. I have had it up to here with you!"

Shep got cocky and whispered in a assertive voice.
"BOOOOHOOOO"

"BOOOHOOO, BOOOHOOOOO! Shep this is Sterling I am going to Fuck you up, you hear me you're a dead man, walk out that door, the snipers are going to kill you!"

Shep had to get this over with the yard was lit now and he was going to see end it win, loose or drawl. Looking out the small diamond window of the front door he scanned the yard, all cool by the driveway. The voices aging it on. "Get your ass out there." "GO, Shep" "Shep he is right there."

He looked toward the tree line on Jonny's side the trailer. The camo was behind the leafless shrub blended well but the shoulders, the arms holding the rifle pointed at the front door were obvious. Shep looked into the trailer adjusting his eyes and back out. Still there the camo brim hat with camo net covering the face that stared back at Shep nodded with an invite. Shep turn the knob and busted out the door, put one hand on the porch rail and leaped over it squatting to break the high fall. He walked, looking dead down the barrel, fist bald by his side, in long stride. Saying very loud "Shoot me motherfucker, Shoot me I ain't scared!" Four strides into it the Sniper's shoulders turned to vines hanging on a small over whelmed sapling the arms turned to limbs and trickery of light, the brim hat a cluster of leaves from a tree that grew some distance behind it. The barrel of the gun a dead limb of the sapling painted black by the morning dew."

"DAMN SHEP good way to get your head blown off by a little tree."

Shep smiled and went backing the house. "I know right, that thing like to have killed me."

They just kept on in the endless conversation. Shep picked the books up off the vents and was going back in his room when Jonny came out his. "What was that all about"

Shep smiled and lied. "Wellll, what happened was, I happened to look out the window and saw that dog you said was strewing your trash fixing to take a shit right there in the drive way. So I ran out there and scared it off."

"I am going to shoot that son of a bitch, I'll do it to"

"That's exactly what I told it. You want to do a line?"

"Might as well."

Him and Jonny spent the better part of the morning passing the foil and snorting lines, talking and fucking with the carburetor on Jonny's old primer grey Chevy truck. Then Shep went to take care of some business.

Chapter 35

The human bug war was on. After refreshing some lawyers memories, Shep took to calling 1-800 numbers and giving his short spill about human bugs. His figuring was the person that answered the phone would tell their family about it then the kids would go to school and tell the class. The husband or wife etc. would tell others. Seems these days mostly foreigners answer the phone. Back then he may call 1-800 for a fitness machine or weight loss add and get some one in Texas, North Dakota, or any other state. The response was something like, "Sounds interesting."

Sometimes he used the computer at his aunts, Deryl's mama's. It was really Andy's computer so he wasn't sure if the E-mails he sent to China, North Korea, or the magazine he found that was all about the mob, ever made it to it's destination. It may have been interpreted by the NSA, being Andy worked at a high security job at the air force base.

Time slipped on to cooler weather. Shep's case in Jones county was being postponed as long as possible by his court appointed attorney. The agents from out of time had settled in to the city of Macon. Martin the CIA agent, Blair the FBI agent and Prep from the DEA were having a good time shooting a game of pool, one night, at a sports bar on Riverside dr. in Macon. Martin's phone rang.

The serious voice on the other end got his attention. "Martin?"

Martin had to speak loud to over shadow the juke box playing The Doors, Break On Through. "This is he!" He headed toward the door into the cool night air and what the air didn't take off his beer buzz the voice did.

"Martin this is your boss."

The traffic of Riverside drive was steady, He passed the parking lot. "Uh, sir yes sir."

"It seems your human bug is trying to e-mail China."

Martin was oblivious to this, he had not been to the cabin in a week or so. Tiffina was on when the e-mail was sent. She was curios to how far the e-mail would make it so didn't say any thing. Shep had thought about it a over a few more shifts and they felt the same way, thinking it was most likely falling on ears that didn't understand English or didn't take it serious.

"Sir I will…" Martin had a realization about it, "Sir, I think now is as good time as any to inform you that we are at war with Shep. He launched a propaganda campaign."

"What the hell martin, why can't you just shut the son of a bitch off?"

"Sir, I feel the best is yet to come."

With some consideration the boss concluded, "I'm not sure how to take that."

"I don't think the world will know how to take it sir, but he's serving it with, take caution."

"Society will in turn feed it to the pigs and the pigs will have it with a side order of crow."

Martin agreed. "Sad but true, I just want to put it all on the table, keep things balanced."

The boss man hummed in decisiveness. "All what the hell, it will give people something to talk about."

"Thank you sir, I'll keep the fire under him."

"I am hungry now Martin, by."

Martin opened the door to the sports bar ready to tell Blair and Prep about the phone call, and his phone rang again. He stepped back into the parking lot. "What's up?"

It was Dumbass sounding calm. "Hey man, y'all wanted to be informed if it looked like something crazy might happen and this could go either way. Shep's on his way to Tiffany's. He had called her on his way in Wal-Mart and got no answer on his way out he tried again, that was about 10:30. She said she just got home and that's why she did not answer the phone the first time, and Marcus was at her sisters. Then before she hung up, she out of know where said She was in the bathroom when he called the first time. She did too, and it's got Shep and us guessing why she did that. He decided to ride up there and make sure she wasn't trying to tell him that somebody was standing there with a gun to her head."

Martin did not want to miss it if Shep was going to try and go Die Hard on some intruder. "What is his ETA?"

"He will be there in about 15."

"We will be there at the cabin about then."

Blair was designated driver, so the other two got one for the road. They loaded into the Crown Vic and Blair turned on the flashing blue grill lights and Martin put one on the dash. The beer was buzzing them into a silly mood and Martin started imitating the three stooges, Prep joined in and Blair turned the radio up on some Red Hot Chile Peppers.

Shep was walking up on Tiffany's high, big front porch listening to the Recluses raise hell, telling Shep he was going to get shot. It was almost

11:00pm. With out being nosey Shep noticed in the narrow glass windows on either side the door the TV was bouncing colors off the walls, past the den the kitchen light was on. He had spent the night there enough to know that the light was off if they were in bed. Shane must be at work his truck is not there.

He knocked on the heavy oak door, thinking there shouldn't be a problem with him checking. He was just over there a few day's ago and spent the day playing with the kids and they washed Tiffany's van for her. She came around the wall the separates the kitchen from the den, Shep could see her from where he stood on the porch though the narrow window. She had on a t-shirt just barely long enough to cover her panties, Shep like to forgot why he was there.

She looked through the glass. Normally she would have opened the door and went back to doing what she was doing, oddly she just looked at him.

Shep made it appoint to sound calm and cool. "Hey I am sorry to show up like this, but on the phone it sounded like something may be wrong. You contradicted yourself about answering the phone the first time."

Her round blue eyes looked like she was opening them wide and several times she looked hard to her right as she said, "Every thing is OK."

"Well since I drove all this way let me in and make sure, I'll be gone in sixty seconds."

"I can't Shane told me not to let anybody in while he is at work." She rolled her eyes over to the right and stopped them there long enough for him to not mistake it.

"Tiffany I understand that but, under the circumstances I think he would understand. I swear I'll just look around and I'm gone." He could see past her. His 3 year old little, curly blond, blue eyed, buddy came walking out from behind the kitchen/den wall, straight down the carpet line separating the kitchen linoleum, took 5 steps turned around and walked straight back behind the wall. It looked to Shep as if he was being told to do it. Shep kept it to himself, just in case, he didn't want to cause any bad guy to take it to another level. "Do this call the kids into the den were I can see you all at once, I'll stay out here."

"No, I am not getting Zack up and Marcus is at my sisters." She paused. "If you don't leave I am going to have to call the law."

"Good when they get here I will be sitting right here on the top step."

She left the door and Shep sat on the step with three new voices putting in their 2cents. "Shep this better be good we left the bar for this." "Don't worry about it Shep his pool game is garbage anyway." "Shep I brought these two stooges…" "Wise guy a" "…with lights flashing and from what I hear on the Bluetooth's we may be in for something."

Shep grunted and thought. "Yea, something, I ought to just kick the door in but you know how that would turn out. I would think she may have a boyfriend in there but not with Mathew up, I'm sure of that. Why is she acting like that, y'all should have seen her eyes she did it on purpose, there is no doubt about that."

During this entire time the rest of the voices in his ear had done their usual, telling him everything from Zack had a gun to his head because she got home and a burglar was in the house, to She had a boyfriend when Shane was at work. Martin said, "Shep my boss was just asking why I don't shut this shit down. This is why Shep, it entertains me, but I told him you had to save the world."

In minutes Shep could see through the woods a Deputy car was on the way the long curvy hill driveway. Before the older white Deputy with a Captain Kangaroo hair cut could ask Shep was explaining. "Look I ain't here to cause any trouble. I had called her to talk to my son and she told me two stories of why she didn't answer the phone the first time and since she said she just got home one of them times. I thought the second stories may have been to tell me something was wrong, like she had come home to somebody in the house."

"Alright you can leave I will handle it from here, She said she don't want you back over here so stay away."

"That is crazy, but I'm leaving I just was worried, I really was." None of this made any since, but what could he do? He got in his truck and was going out the driveway looking in the rear view. The Deputy was behind him, in his car. Shep thought, to the Recluses who had not let up with murderess plots. "I should have kicked the door in, ya' reckon? That mother fucker ain't had time to spit much less make sure things was secure."

"Damn it Shep now we don't know why she acted like that." "Shep I fuckin tell you man, I got half a mind to go to Tiffany's and kick the door in myself." "Man this sux Shep I would have stayed at the bar if I had known you was just going to make me worry bout' them kids." Shep I just heard a 911 call on the scanner every thing is not OK………."

Shep made one more attempt to save their ass. When he cleared the Jones County line he stopped and called the Sheriffs office. A mans voice, "Jones County Sheriffs Department, Mandia, how may I help you?" Mandia was already familiar with Shep and his Human Bug theory. He had got the low on it when Shep was locked up for the terrorist threat. He said he had worked with Sterling on the drug squad and it sounded like something he would do and it would not suprize him if the technology was possible, but he was betting that Shep had fried his brain.

"Hey Mandia this is Shep, the human bug."

"I know who you are Shep."

Shep gave him the run down on what had happened. He said he was fixing to clock out in just a minute and he personally would ride over there and make sure all was secure. He sounded sincere but Shep got the feeling he just didn't want him to worry.

It was a long night for Shep in his bed room staring at the dark ceiling. He didn't need the Recluses to make him worry himself sick, but they killed her and the kids everyway imaginable, saying they was just being good sports about it.

The next day Shep's love for others would get him in such a mess it just don't make sense, and folks say, why did you do that?" It is a fool that looks for logic in the chambers of the human heart. He was following his heart.

Chapter 36

The time was about 3pm. The day peaceful, sun shining, not too hot not too cold. Shep knew he had arrived early, Tiffany wouldn't be home yet. He was pleased to see Shane's black Toyota truck in the driveway. The sound of a vacuum cleaner from in the house became clear as he climbed the front steps.

A voice in his ear added to the one sided topics, "Shep he's cleaning up all the blood and guts from last night. You should have never left the house insecure."

Shep whispered out loud as he pushed the Big Bear folded knife case further around his back, out of sight. "I just want to let him know that I am their friend."

Knocking loud, so it could be heard over the vacuum, he could see Shane 6 ft. from the door vacuuming the den floor. Shane ignored the knocking. Shep knocked louder to make sure Shane heard it, even though he knew the first had to be heard. Shane kept his eyes on the floor and ignored Shep. All parties involved on Shep's end agreed that something had happened and Shep was getting the cold shoulder because of it.

He decided Shane was not the one to take this up with on account Shane would not acknowledge his presence. Taking his leave he went down the dirt road Tiffany and Shane lived on to a friend of his the same age called Babba. He was a big boy, round face sported a clean cut goatee. Shep knew him from way back when they hung at a bar called The Final Chapter, in 91' - 93'.

Bubba slowly rocked on the full house length front porch of the two story house, nice, the electrical union had been good to Babba. Shep was rocking his own chair, both sipping on their beer. He was explaining to Bubba the goings on of the night before and the latest developments.

Bubba reflected. "Buddy, I tell ya' seems odd to me too and I can understand your dilemma. You shoulda' kicked the door in."

"Yea hind site is 20/20."

The Recluses had multiplied. All waiting for this thing to play through, and they had nothing better to do. So Sterling and Tiffina and Scooter sat at the cabin with the two that had came back from the night before one being Dumbass and the four that had the shift. All letting opinions fly into Shep's ears. Shep kept his cool. He had stopped in and talked to Bubba a number of times since the voices had started. Bubba was opened minded about the agents, or as he called them "Them fed's in yo' head."

Shane's truck went by kicking the dust up on his way out to work. Shep informed the cabin out loud. "There go's Shane."

Bubba confirmed it. "Yep."

Shep pointed out 30 seconds later. "And there go's Tiffany on her way home." as the burgundy Astro van came speeding by.

Bubba slowly turned his head and looked at him with a questioning look. "Yep?"

"Hell you know I can't just let this go." Heading for his 73' Chevy Shep asked for luck.

"Good luck."

Shep came up Tiffany's long, dirt, hilly, driveway, taking his time. Knocking on the door with them still raising hell, he was not angry at all, he saw no reason to be. He wanted to just step away, but he had done got attached, his brain said let it alone his heart said why?" She came to the door and spoke through the window as she did the night before. "I can't let you in."

"I don't want in."

"Well you better leave the law is on the way."

"I just wanted you to know I love y'all and Shane's cool by me, I was really worried about y'all and just wish you would have let me see y'all through the window so I'd known y'all were OK. I'm don't want to cause any trouble."

She yelled, "Boys come in here." Zack and Mathew came into view, she added, "Marcus is still at my sisters."

He rolled his eyes and smiled shook his head. "Thank you." With that he returned to his truck, and slowly started pulling away. He had not got out the parking area good, when a new black Chevy Malibu with blue lights in the front grill, not flashing but noticeable, pulled into the parking area with no attempt to stop Shep's old truck.

Shep was hearing the cabin, reflect on the situation with, "Fuck that mother fucker Shep haul ass."

Hind site is 20/20. Shep put the truck in reverse, not wanting this to turn into a one sided story that made him look like a deranged lunatic. The tall, lanky, young detective maybe 26, in street clothes, had short brown hair and noticeable brown eyes. Shep being a man wondered if Tiffany was fucking him, not that he cared, but it crossed his mind. He leaned on the car at drivers side back door and crossed his arms over his chest as Shep stood 10 ft. away explaining his reason for being there from the beginning of it all the night before, including he had just been there a few days before and had no problems.

The detect whom happened to be kin folk of the Sheriff of Jones County, had no hesitation. "That sounds reasonable man. Look they want you to stay away for some reason or another, and it would be best if you waited till you were invited back."

As the detect was telling Shep this a Deputy car was hauling ass in their direction, no sirens or blue lights just the sound of the throttle being pumped and the wash outs in the drive way.

Shep was saying, "I ain't got a problem with that, I don't want to cause….."

The Deputy car slammed on the brakes and slid up behind the detect car. The 280 lbs. of Deputy was shortening the six steps between his self and Shep fast and in a hurry, with orders for Shep to keep his hands where he could see them.

Shep's hands being raised, palms up in question to the detect, who seemed to be as surprised as Shep. It was too fast for explanation, the Deputy stuck his right foot behind Shep's feet, at the same time plowed into him with his shoulder. Tripping backwards Shep rolled on the way to the ground, landing on his chest. The Deputy planted his knee in the center of his back, trapping his arm to the ground. "Put your hands behind your back!"

"My arms trapped, my arms trapped!"

"Put your hands behind your back!"

The detect was objecting. "Travis what the hell are you doing, what the hell man!?"

Shep was stuck. "Get your fat ass off me!"

Crazy but Shep was so used to the voices talking non stop he brought it to the cabins attention that they had got so caught up in what as happening they were speechless trying to take it all in. Shep was told by a voice in his ear, "Shut up Shep we trying to hear what's happening!"

Shep heard a click and heard the spray as the back of his head became soaked in spray, not just a squirt, it was the whole damn can of pepper spray.

The Deputy backed off coughing and gagging. The detect noticed the knife on Shep's belt pushed around to his back and stepped in removing it. Stedly cussing the Deputy. "God damn man, he was not hurting anything, I had this situation under control!"

Shep was trying to lift up off the ground when the Deputy grabbed his arms and pulled them behind him and cuffed him. Shep still had not felt the spray that was irritating the detect and the Deputy. Another Deputy car parked. The arresting officer was still taking the heat from the detect and protested "I work the streets and I ain't taking any chances." He turned to the Deputy that had just arrived on the scene. "Take him to the LEC for me I can't see I got pepper spray in my eyes."

Tiffany came on to the porch. "What the hell are y'all doing, everybody out of my yard, all of you get the hell out of my yard!"

Shep was put in the back of the car. His sweat glands opened up and the pepper spray took root. "HOLY SHIT I AM ON FIRE!" That's what it felt like too, he had been put in a fire and held there. The Recluses joined back in with no sympathy for his situation. The spray had soaked his head ran down his back his chest all the way between his legs. He tried to hold the pain in but it overpowered him. He cussed the world for all it was worth. The Deputy driving the car sympathized and rolled down all the windows saying he could not hold his eyes open due to the fumes and kept telling Shep, "I am hurrying man we gonna' get that shit washed off you, Damn he got you good."

Shep disagreed. "I don't see nothing good about it, MY BALLS ARE ON FIRE, I am going to die, I cant breath, I'm on fire, Fuck I ain't never felt nothing like this!" He tried to open his eyes but they refused to open clamping shut as tight as they could from the burn. His skin felt like it was being skinned. It can't really be put in to words what a full can of pepper spray feels like."

At the LEC getting out the car, forever later it seemed, Shep's sinuses had opened up and two long, and this is pretty gross, two strands of snot swung from his nostrils to below his waste like thick rope refusing to stretch or break. He felt embarrassed as another Deputy came from with in the LEC to see.

His chauffer told the new Deputy to get some of the blue shop towels from his car console and give them to Shep as he uncuffed him.

Shep was still damn near out of his mind on fire, he wiped the swinging rope from his nose and couldn't help smiling at the mess he had done got his self into. "I'm burning." is all he could say.

They led him and the loud voices in his ear, into the building down a hall. Shep trying to open his eyes to see where he was, caught a glimpse of Mandia headed out the doors they had just entered, he looked pissed off. "Where is Travis?" He ordered.

"I think he was on the way here."

Mandia went outside. Shep was put in the intake shower and told to wait there some body was going to help him. Shep was so burning he knew that the only thing that was going to help him was time. He had uncontrollably started humming short "hummmmmm, hummmm, hummmmmm" over and over a natural meditation reflex that tries to separate our minds from the pain of our physical. It wasn't working. Neither did the spray that Mandia sprayed him down with before and after he stripped naked and was left in the shower for 20 minutes, He was on fire, the shower seemed to make it worse but turning off the shower didn't help either.

Mandia kept check on him. "This should not have happened to you man, I know you meant well. Travis needs his ass kicked."

All Shep could say was "I'm on fire." hummmmming.

Two hours later the burning was giving way to a shivering cold from the inside out. The mat he laid on in solitary confinement felt familiar from not to long ago. The voices stories sounded familiar also. They all thanked him for not letting them down by delivering one hell of an unexpected show.

Shep accepted it as though he was accepting an Academy Award, saying out loud in his solitude. "I would like to thank my fans and I could not have did this with out the love form my friends.........."

After midnight a young girl officer with big glasses that magnified her brown eyes and a plump ass retrieved Shep to do some paper work.

Shep exited the solitary room with a joke. "This has all been a misunderstanding, I'll take my clothes now and get out yall's way."

"I'm afraid not your being charged with felony obstruction of an officer and criminal trespassing. You should know better than try and pull a knife on an officer."

Shep felt a sinking feeling in his gut, this was going to be a lot more series than he thought, and he was stuck looking crazy. "That son of a bitch.

That's how it's going down, just flat out lie" He knew explaining to this jail officer was pointless. He went through the booking process, Tiffina was their in his ear to hold his hand as the others kicked him. She said "Shep it don't get much lower than that, using somebody's love against them."

Shep was feeling it, he Bluetoothed back. "I know baby, I could see if I was acting like a stalker or like I was irrational, but all was cool a few day's ago and she gave me them looks like on purpose through the window, I kinda' feel like I was set up, but why?"

And the voices had no shortage of reasons why and Shep had no shortage of time in solitary to listen. "Shep was a scape goat for Shane. He killed somebody and he buried the body he is going to pin it on you." That story went all kinda direction's. "Shep they were forced to join the KKK and this was part of their initiation to set you up……….." On and on and on.

Chapter 37

The 8x10 cell was not getting any bigger and it was awfully crowded with him and the Recluses in it, so on the 15th day when the court sent him back to Central State hospital he was glad to go. Going home would have been better.

His parents came to visit him at the mental institution and unlike last time they brought him some clothing so he didn't have to wear the homeless had me downs. He got the speech of "You need to get your life together,". They had gathered from Tiffany that he was over at her house acting crazy and high and she was just trying to get him some help. Of course they found his version of the story unlikely because he was on drugs. They felt like if he would get off the meth the voices would go away. They must not be able to add, because if taken into account the way the voices became 24/7 every second when he had been locked in that place for five months,,, it just didn't add up to the voices going away.

Shep missed the Jody Foster shrink from South Carolina and not being a coed facility no chance of another Amanda encounter. The psychiatrist was a young man from India. Shep started giving him the human bug experience starting with the technology of it, and that's as far as he got.

The Doc said in his broken English, "This is normal for to think maybe computer chips in your brain."

Shep was amazed at how people could hear things in such detail and totally twist it into what they wanted to hear. He had said nothing about computer chips. He didn't expect the man to accept the theory as rational, he just was hoping for some better reaction than getting totally wrong. He was prescribed the anti-psycho meds, which he had no intention of taking.

Nothing much had changed at the loony bin. He found his place in the unused dayroom, as last time, and was run out when ever the wrong staff found him there. He spit his meds out. Laid on his bed and in the constant conversation state of mind thinking thing s like, he wanted some meth, the time in Jones County LEC and the two weeks he had already been there had sucked the life out of him. He wanted to go back to work. But he was stuck and watching shows like, Monk, Regis and Kelly, Law & Order, not being able to pay all that close attention to them. This was his entertainment. So much for being a hero.

Being a hero? That was the question, to be or not to be. That was on his mind a lot. One voice said if he had kicked that fucking door in he would be a hero. Shep was bothered by this, what had went wrong? He was not looking to be a hero. The situation had pulled him into it and although he did not kick the door in he cared enough to sit on the steps and wait on the law, just in case Tiffany's actions were because of a hostage situation. Even knowing the unlikelihood of it.

One evening as he came down the hall he seized an opportunity. The nurse station had been left unattended and there sat the phone. He gave a quick look around into the dayroom that had a few patients zoned into the TV, the hall was clear. Ducking behind the desk he grabbed the phone and knelt down under it. Guessing 9 to get an out side line he got a dial tone.

867-5309 He called Tiffany she answered. "Hello"

"Hey this is Shep I don't know why y'all are turning me away, I want you to know that for what ever reason I guess you had to do it, just tell the kids I love them and wish things were different."

"I will. Ain't you supposed to be in Central State?"

"I am. I am hiding under the nurses desk. She's gone some where."

"OH my god, you are so damn crazy, really."

"Yea really, I am glad that nothing was wrong that night, I got to get off this phone talk to you later."

"OK, behave yourself."

Shep set the phone backup on the desk as he stood, hoping no nurse would be in sight. None was seen. He was getting mixed reviews from the voices, he was fixing to get busted the whole time he was under the desk, and the other two on shift gave him props for doing it.

One of the agents went as far as. "Man that's why I hate this shit, y'all don't see how cool that was. That was awesome Shep keep up the good work."

He felt better it took a lot off his mind making the call. The agents talked about him about being jobless and people he knew getting busted, and even had a great discussion about quantum physics and things of that nature with the whittle till sleep came. He slept for a good 5 hours straight that night. Wakening to at least 2 minutes of silence in the morning. By far the most silence he had since Sue had picked him up.

"Shep don't get used to it we………….." on and on and on………

Chapter 38

Sitting in the day room Shep was slightly depressed Christmas had came and gone. Dumbass's voice not making it any better with the talk of how useless Shep was not being home for his Parent's and the kids. Shep reminded himself that he was doing just fine till that stunt Tiffany pulled, it helped shed some of the blame.

He set his mind on the human bug war for the millionth time since he had gotten to the loony bin. Telling folks around there was pointless he didn't even attempt it, most were so far gone they couldn't comprehend such a story. When he got out of there a simple propaganda strategy would be to write about it on bathroom stall walls. It may be taken as a joke but at least somebody might be talking about it. A short message like,,,AM crystal radio nano size in food attached to nerves system, walking walky-talkies. That was short.

"Shep that don't even make any fucking since you stupid fuck." "Yea Shep you need more detail." No what he needs is to be kept in that nut house." "This ain't 12 Monkey's Shep."

Shep had made up his mind. Even thinking that the nanobugs more than likely were not possible today he had to do something to warn the public about the fact that it will be done in the not so distant future. He had to do something for the kids of tomorrow, to protect them from Big Brother. He knew it was just a matter of time. The mind reading maybe a thousand years or more but the simple listening and talking to people via nanobugs that had been put in their food or drink, that was maybe possible today. Just a matter of time.

The panel of doctors and counselors told Shep in a meeting with them that they felt it in his best interest if he filed for disability and social security. They would help him get it started. He decided right then, in the meeting, that if he was waiting on a check it would take away a part of his oomph, his get up and go. In doing so the flames that Sterling had lit behind him would engulf him. He turned it down. (A year and half later he would realize that had been a foolish thing to do, because they never shut up;-)

It was a long four months at the loony bin castle but his day of release finally came. His dad picked him up and took him home. Gave him a place to stay and fed him till he could get back on his feet. They can be the greatest parents in the world. He went to Jonny's, his last place of residents, who had moved a girl in with him and needed no company any how, and picked up his boxes of stuff.

Shep landed another job two weeks after he got home. The Sheet metal specialist did artsy things, like chandeliers and other pretty stuff but kept the machine rolling by doing small sub work for companies like Metal Concepts. The boss was cool, not meth or drug cool but cool. Things like that made it, not bearable, but a smite more bearable having to deal with the 24/ every second agents. He did not tell the new boss about them, but was told to pay attention a lot.

It was about the same time his parents Frank and Louise went to Savanna, on the Georgia coast for the weekend. Spring had sprung. When they came home his dad packed for an extended stay and went back. He had struck up a conversation with a man working on a nice sized cabin curser. The boat was donated to a group of Seventh Day Evangelist by the coast guard in order for it to be used to go to islands off the Pacific South American coast to treat the less fortunate with Doctor care. Frank had talked himself into helping get the boat sea ready.

Frank was born in and left Wilmington North Carolina to go to the Army. He shortly found himself in Vietnam. Tank division, a leader in his platoon, getting blown out of a tank he received a Purple Heart, recovered from his injuries, all but his hearing, that has dwindled to barely. On his way home he stopped in Macon, Georgia to see his brother and was set up on a date with Shep's mamma. He never made it back to North Carolina. This Boat was his childhood back.

Louise went to Savanna to visit him every so often during the month or so he worked on the boat. When it took leave of port Frank sailed off with it. They cut across the Panama Canal and back up the west coast.

Frank being a Hell fire brimstone Baptist and the two others on the boat being Seventh Day Evangelist gave Shep and the Recluses quite a few scenarios to pass the time back in Dry Branch. "Shep they through your dad over board because he would not stop preaching about them going to hell." "Shep your dad just set the boat on fire trying to prove his Baptist God was the only God, praying to be saved." It was humorous for the most part.

They reached the West Coast and Louise flew out to be with Frank. The boat picked up some Doctors and such and continued on the mission. A trip Shep's parents had no desire to take. Touring the West Coast led to a trip to Hawaii. They liked it, got jobs, an apartment and stayed.

When Louise had boarded the plane back in Georgia, Shep had to find a place to live, besides his parents house. The truck transmission had lost reverse, so as he drove up the hill of the gravel driveway that curved to the right and finally at the top of the hill he saw it continued on back to the road, He recognized, "No Reverse, horse shoe drive way, it must be meant to be."

"Shep this girl you have not seen in over a year and you think she is going to let you move in?" "Shep, she knows you just got out the loony bin and….." "Shep fuck all that, what's this chick look like, all you keep Bluetoothing is "Brown eyed beauty with a little soft booty."

The double wide trailer was an older model. Shep stood on the big, carpeted, screened in front porch, surrounded by hanging ferns and potted

plants doing well in the warm climate. A rapid loud knock on the door soon
was returned with Tammy's voice, she talked through her nose. "Who is it?"

Shep got to the point. "Your new room mate."

The door opened and stood a 35 year old short and thin, naturally tan
skin, brown hair, loosely curly past her shoulders, pretty lil' fairy tittys
showing braless in her sleeveless tie die shirt, her cut off sweat pants hugged
her tight. She looked him up and down scowling "I don't let strangers move
in with me."

He had known her since the Meth dealing days of the Final Chapter
where she was a bar tender. They quickly became best of friends and found
it ran a lot a lot deeper when being friends just wasn't enough some nights.

Before he made a move he cleared a few things up. "You got a
boyfriend?"

Rolling her eyes, she pouted, "No."

Shep stepped into the doorway and picked her up grabbing her ass as
she rapped her legs around his waist. They kissed hard and long, stopping to
look each other in the eyes and smile.

Shep imposed. "looks like you got yourself a new roommate."

She shook her head. "you think you can…"

Shep saw the bed room door opened. The trailer was neat and clean
but cluttered with nick knack, vases, duck figurines, decretive plates with

pics of Jesus and poems on them, and old deco style lamps, it looked like a flash back yard sale. He carried her to the bedroom.

She protested. "No, you ain't." But grinded her hips into his.

Kissing her, He laid her on the bed. The next morning he broke from her embrace and retrieved his tote of clothes from his truck.

Chapter 39

A few weeks after moving in with Tammy an old friend of Shep's stopped by. This was a surprise for Shep. He didn't know they knew each other.

Dell a short, blond dude, still looking like a kid, stepped into the trailer. "Shepsy Pepsy." He had always said a rhyme with Shep's name.

Shep smiled as the memories were pictured of the preteen days of growing up on Gailu Dr. with his best friend. All the dragons and trolls they slayed in the dead cornfields past the end of the street.

Dell asked Shep, "You hit'en that?" with a motion of his head toward Tammy who was listening from the kitchen.

She let out a "Hummm" at Dell's candidness.

Shep was honest. "Hell yea, are you?"

From the kitchen Shep got a look of scorn. "Ahhhhh!"

Dell shook his head. "Fraid not, my brother used too."

She laughed and sighed. "I hate y'all, and your brother ain't never hit this."

Dell started informing Shep. "I'm on the way out to Stan's. I always stop by here to see if she has a joint."

The coincidence was Sterling had been in Shep's ears all morning. He knew Dell from Gailu dr. and had a story for Shep. "Dell's working for me now Shep, I told him where to find you and...."

Shep shrugged it off thinking. "Gee thanks Sterling I mist my old buddy" This fired the cabin up and they cussed Shep for being a smart ass and pretty much kept to Dell, confidential informant stories the rest of the afternoon.

He questioned Dell. "Stan's?" Stan was a name he had not heard in a while. He was the same age as Shep and Dell and grew up across the street from the store Shep's family had owned. From a distance he looked like Shep.

"Yea, he's living on the far side of the county, cooking that good shit. Are you still fucking with it?"

"Dose a cat got climbing gear?"

Dell lit up. "Might save me a trip."

Shep disappointed him. "Naw, scrounged up the last little bit for me and her last night. Let me go to Stan's with you, I need a new connection."

Dell went out the door. "Well lets go I'm in a hurry."

Shep reminded him about the joint and Dell kept moving toward the van that looked style and paint wise like the A-Team van. "I already got some, I was just looking for a freebee."

Tammy hugged Shep by with a kiss to the cheek, whispering in his ear "Be careful."

It was a trip clean across the county to Stan's so they had plenty of time to catch up on things. Shep noticed how fast the van was moving down Hwy. 80. "What's the hurry?"

I got to get home before my old lady gets off work, so by the time I get out here and back to the other side of Macon I will be cutting it close. She got another baby in the oven and been raising hell about every thing I do."

"Can't blame her."

"Me either, but....you know. I got a job interview tomorrow with a roofing company, you want to go to work?"

Shep had lost his job at the sheet metal place a week ago, for bei9ng late all the time. "No, I got them voices in my ears and I would just end up loosing it. I got to find something but I guess I will just deal meth till something better comes along."

Dell reflected. "The last time I saw you was living next door to Deryl's. You was talking about Sterling being at your window and then you disappeared."

Shep filled him in on what had happened till they pulled into a driveway with a cow gate across it. Shep got out and opened the gate and closed it behind them. Stan was doing it big compare to Shep. Cooking five ounces or more a month. Stan had went up to Atlanta and found a company with big freezers that used Anhydrous Ammonia, as a refrigerant, instead of Freon. It was risky but he was able to fill tanks up under the cover of darkness and bring them home. He and Shep hit it off good, finding out that Stan had learned the process from a guy that learned it from a guy that learned it from Gabby who Shep set the spark with. Stan was paying off his mom's land for her, it was fairly big heavy wooded. He had a cool two story cabin toward the back for his two sons 10 and 8 and his wife.

Shep got a 8ball and was invited back. Shep returned a few days later starting a habit of bringing cold pills to add to the mix and other necessities. He and Stan mixed it all together, Shep showed him a few short cuts. It was good out there in the woods, Shep liked it. The agents fucked with him hard, throwing their voices from the woods, and all didn't freak him out, but it did keep him alert. Stan was not sure what to think of the voices. Sometimes talking about them like he kinda' believed Shep was a human bug, but not enough to stop the flow of things.

Shep met a girl over there, Cristal another girl he had first met at the Final Chapter. She was very short, thin, bottle blond hair, and green eyes that glowed, and a little every thing, nose, ears etc. Shep wanted her so bad. They started hanging out together. Also he met another chick that was 19 over at someone else's house. Eava, had short brown hair and round brown eyes and fairly big breast to mach her ass. Her and Cristal and Shep spent a lot of time together. Tammy knew it was the nature of the beast, and was cool with it, but she would not tolerate Shep bringing anybody home to spend the night.

The dealing grew more and more, making Tammy more and more paranoid. The broke mirrors standing around the yard was a clue. She had to see everywhere. When he came home with the story of where he had been one day, she couldn't take it any more and after four months of Shep, he had to go.

Chapter 40

The human bug war story that broke Tammy's back was this:

Shep couldn't believe he was on his way to do this, but the voices had been raising so much hell for so long, he had to do something drastic to level the playing field, so to speak. Seeing what the voices in his ear looked like, if real, made since.

He parked in the parking garage after finding a place that was on a down hill slope. Breaking a sweat as walked into the huge office building, on out Riverside dr. and I-75. He asked where to find the DEA office, listening to the agents in his ear. "Shep we ain't even at the office we are at the cabin." "I am at the office Shep." "Me too, come on up here." "He's bluffing anyway, I think." Shep was thinking of going back to his truck but kept moving to the elevator.

On the third floor he walked into the DEA office instantly thinking, "I want that copper sailing ship on the wall. It's awesome. Be hard to walk out of here with it, I'm sure."

"Shep, Shep, Shep, I have been thinking the same thing for years."

Behind a small glass window in the wall, atop a small counter, sat a Latina looking girl, dark skin, skinny, jet black hair, pulled tight to a pony tail.

He made eye contact. "I would like to speak with someone in charge."

A male voice in his ear responded. "Hold on Shep I'll be right there." The Latina chick just nodded stood then disappeared through a door.

He found a seat in the small waiting area. Noticing that the girl did not speak, his conspiracy thinking considered it may be Tiffina, not wanting him to recognize her voice. He had always pictured her looking more thicker, a blond.

Tiffina's voice suddenly hit his ear. "There is a lot of things you think about us that you are wrong about." Just before she finished saying it the Latina girl came back into view.

Shep concluded with voice masking technology they could do each others voice at any time. He couldn't believe he was fixing to talk to the DEA about some mind reading technology. Leaving that part out would be best, he decided. This was not about him, it was about the possibility of real human bugs.

Dumbass's voice came to him in the usual more than hateful way. "What the fuck are you doing Shep!? We are fixing to lock you up."

A middle aged man wearing Dockers pants a blue Polo pull over and penny loafers opened the door opposite the entrance door and looked into the waiting room. "May I help you?"

"I needed to talk to some body about...." He paused lost for words. ".....about some crazy stuff that has been happening."

The agent invited him to the other side the door into a small interviewing room with a small table, three chairs, and a filing cabinet.

He took a seat as the agent remained standing, leaning on the wall by another door. Shep jumped into his story. "I have a friend that has been hearing voices in his ear, and I have been there when..."

The agent stopped him. "Hold up a second man. I got some others that want to hear this." He left into a hall of unpainted cement blocks and a concrete floor. Returning with three more agents, dressed like him for the most part, same age, except for a younger one that had a old school mushroom preppy hair cut.

The voices had been going with, Shep was barking up the wrong tree suddenly switched to. "You got us Shep, that is us." "That ain't me Shep but that is some Recluses standing before you." Dumbass's voice warned loudly. "Get a good look, cause we are the last ones you will see when we lock your ass up."

Starting over with the story Shep told them he was witness to his friend saying that the voices had been saying that something was going on somewhere else and the voices had got it right one to many times for the law of probability. "I think it could possibly be nanotechnology...."

The agent that had greeted him, stopped him again. "Hold on there, I've got someone that you need to tell this to." He disappeared down the hallway.

Shep decided to affiliate himself with them better. "I grew up on the same street with Sterling so…."

The agent returned in time to hear the Sterling plug. They all just nodded. Following the agent into the room came what looked to be the youngest of them all, or maybe it was the Iron Maiden "Peace of Mind" T shirt, his skinniness only exaggerated by way tight jeans, shoulder length frizzy hair that framed a rat face. He walked in the room like he had just ate a bowl of Cherries to find out it had been pissed in.

One of the agents introduced him. "This is our gadget guy he works on our technical stuff, computers, cameras."

Shep was thinking he looked like a nark from 1980 something. The voice in his ear that stood out was Tiffina's. "That's him Shep, Punch him in the nose."

The nark looking one did a perfect impression of Dumbass, the voice the attitude, as he started yelling at Shep with body language almost to the point of stomping. "What is this shit your talking about!"

Shep didn't quiver he just stayed cool. "This friend of mine is hearing voices in his ear and they say they are you, I think it may be nanotechnology."

This seemed to piss the gadget guy off even more. "You don't know anything about nanotechnology!" He calmed down just a hair. The problem is they have no way to power nano….bots."

"If it is AM crystal radios on a nano scale it would not need batteries to receive and as far as y'all listening, the nervous system could power that."

The Gadget guy looked at the other agents, "This guy needs to lay off the dope, he needs to be in a mental institution." He looked at Shep "Why would we do that to your friend that is just stupid." Marching out the door "y'all lock him up!" As if he had the final word in everything.

Shep looked at the agents. "Emotional ain't he.,"

The agent that had greeted him asked, "You ain't going to hurt anybody or yourself are you. I mean it seems like you know what your talking about as far as the technology?"

"Naw man, I just know what I saw my friend do, and it got me thinking."

The prep agent tried to trip Shep up. "So, about this friend of yours, why would we be interested in him anyway?"

"Crazy thing is, he was into meth real big but the voices done got him walking the line, in church every Sunday."

The greeting agent was satisfied with that. "OK, stay out of trouble, don't do anything to hurt anybody." He showed Shep into the hallway of cement bare block walls and to a door that led him out to the elevator.

"Shep I wish I was at the office today, you would not have gotten off that easy." "I am there, Shep, I was just standing right in front of you." Dumbass's voice. "SHEP I can not believe you got away! You should be locked up! But now you walked in here and gave us a real lead, we can't use the info we get from the bugs in you to get anybody, you just gave us a good reason to keep an eye on you."

He got in his truck and then got back out. Standing in the door he gave it a hard push backwards to get it rolling down the hill, coasting far enough back he crunk it up and off he went.

"Shep no you ain't. You just barely walked out of the DEA office and now you are going to try your luck at the FBI office." "Shep I don't know how often that happens, skitso's walking into the this guy's office asking question's…." "That's the first time in the eight years I been there" "Shep they tell me it don't happen a whole hellava' lot. But what I was saying was at the MIB office you would not have made it in the front door, you would not have found the front door, it has a magic force field around it that makes it invisible." Everybody at the cabin and Shep driving down Riverside dr. laughed a little smile at that.

Dumbass started raising hell again then a voice (and Shep imagined this was a staged presentation, if they was real) a voice interrupted him as though it had just walked into the room pissed off. "What the fuck was that all about you dumbass! You just gave us away, you don't have any idea how stupid that was!"

Dumbass tried to argue. "I don't give a fuck, what is that dope head going to…."

"There is a hell of a lot he can do about it, for instance he could, he could, go ahead Shep tell this Dumbass what your going to do about it.!"

Shep slowed down to a stop at a red light. "I'll tell Dumbass what I am fixing to do about it. Dumbass I am going to the FBI office and tell them you are….Americas most wanted, to put you at the top of the list." Shep was hoping the FBI office was still downtown where he had read the office number legend in a elevator. He was using the bank that is in the same building.

"Shep the local FBI is in on it to, they sit right here in this cabin…." A loud whisper as meaning to be heard. "I'm in the office man remember, that's what I told him." "Look Shep where ever we are the FBI is in on it."

"Well, I reckon I am going to talk to some more folks that talk to me. It don't matter if your all just a part of my brain done split into a bunch of Recluses, or if your real people, doing this is for the kids of tomorrow. I just might get lucky and warn the right person or somebody I tell may warn the right person and BAM! I saved the world. Other than that it is more exciting than staring at the wall talking to y'all." He pulled all the way in a parking spot so he could drive forward out of it. The BB&T office building is 8 stories high and takes up a quarter of a block.

As he entered the building the voices told him how crazy he was. Shep Bluetoothed back to them. "Dumbass your going down man. Your going down like a dick sucking clown."

"Shep I hope you don't think your going to call me Dumbass from now on. I am the Gadget Guy, you retard. Just keep calling me Dumbass, I will turn this thing up till your head explodes."

He pushed the 5th floor button, the doors closed, "Dumbass,,,, I'll make ya' famous."

Chapter 41

The FBI office on the 5th floor of the BB&T building had a small waiting room and that's where the similarities between it and the DEA office stopped. There was no ship on the wall, the commercial grade blue carpet gave it a more relaxed feel. Behind the sliding glass window partition there was no one to great him. He made use of the tap bell on the window ledge. Ding, Ding, Ding, Ding.

Over the yadee, yadee, yada of Dumbass and the rest of the gang, Scooter's voice rang in his ears as if by the magic of the bell. "Shep this is Scooter, I got a call saying you were off the chain."

Shep thought. "Yea man, you know drastic times call for drastic measures."

Tiffina's voice, "I hear ya' Shep you go boy. We are at the beach in south Florida, and by we I mean me and Scooter."

Shep had two thoughts over laying each other and both came loud and clear to Scooter and Tiffina as they sat on beach towels with the tide rolling in and out at their feet. On a cooler a bug phone sat between them. "What the fuck ever." at the same time "I'm jealous."

Shep had a soft spot in his heart for Tiffina. He knew how crazy it was, being she was most likely a voice created by his own brain. It was times like these she seemed she was much more than a voice. Imagine standing in the FBI office, mind totally fixed on the situation. The voices from the cabin and maybe the DEA office compounding it. Your not thinking about some folks sitting on a beach in Florida, and yet there they are.

Scooter continued. "I am glad they picked you to bug Shep. You keep things interesting. "What you fixing to tell the FBI agents?"

Tiffina butted in. "Shep you want to hear the ocean? Let me turn up your volume."

The agent's in Macon beckoned to hear the sound. "I want to hear it." "Me too." "Shep be quiet so we can hear the ocean."

Shep tried to clear his thoughts and think absolutely nothing, it was imposable. He already knew, from the past that thinking of thinking of nothing is thinking. With no talk from the Recluses for five seconds he was able to hear the ebb and flow of waves crashing. It was a sweet five seconds that ended with the door opening that led to the rest of the FBI office, and the voices picking back up with him going to the loony bin.

The slightly big in the waist and height, five o' clock shadow, mullet hair cut, jeans and a cheap button down shirt, tennis shoes, 50 years of age, FBI agent was comical. "You rannngg?" as if a butler of a haunted house.

Shep felt like he could talk to this guy straight up. "Uh, yes sir. I needed to talk to somebody about some illegal surveillance."

Scooter applauded. "Great start Shep."

The FBI agent asked as if it routine, waving him to join him through the doorway. "Why would that concern us?"

Shep thought, "I'm a fucking geniuses." as he answered the agent. " I think they are doing it from across state lines."

On the other side the door, now occupied by three people, including Shep, it was one big room with nine desk greatly separated, a high tile ceiling made it seem much more empty. The massive wall of window stretched the length of the office and turned left to the next wall, giving a five story view of the Ocmulgee river to the left and the top of the building across the street.

The other agent in the office was about Shep's size, 50 ish, dressed in regular old street clothes, his round head sported a Gilligan kinda hat, but brown, looked right with his thick gasses.

The larger agent introduced himself. "I'm Agent Thompson and this is Agent Poindexter. We have an interview room this way." Shep was showed to a 12x12 room that was built inside the big room with the desks. The heat and air duct work and 1 inch electrical conduit could be seen dropping into the ceiling of the small room.

Once through the cheap wood door with a small square window, they took seats on the appropriate sides of the heavy wood office desk. Shep came out with it. "I think the local DEA are making human bugs, walking walky-talkies."

The FBI agent that had greeted him chuckled. "Sounds like some crap they would do."

"I think they did it to me."

"Why?"

Shep avoided the twist of the question, the part about why did they bug him, and went with the, Why he thought he was a human bug. "I hear voices in my ear not my head, and I came up with this nanotechnology theory. It's AM crystal radios on a nano scale attached to an amino acid or something that will combine with the nervous system like some snake venoms, and since there are billions and billions of them, the nano crystals vibrate to send electrical signals of sound to the listeners and I can hear them because the AM radio vibrates crystals in the nerve hairs in my ear that's why they sound from the outside in."

Poindexter just sat in a chair behind the desk but in the corner and Thompson leaned back in his office chair, crossing his arms. "What are they saying, and why you?"

They said they are going to kill me or make me stronger by talking nonstop till they, for any reason have to shutdown, or I kill myself. See the FBI and CIA came from D.C. to investigate my cuz for a job at the U.S. embassy in Russia, in maintenance. That same week, my friend DEA agent Sterling was pissed at me. y'all know him?"

Slow nods of affirmative

Shep went on. "Any way I started hearing people at my window that week saying the was gonna stick a baseball bat up my ass if I went to sleep. Called themselves the Brown Recluses, It was Sterling and the two from D.C., they said they was anyway. They was going to scare me to my senses. I'm just gonna' skip to, they was not at my window, they was in my ear. Said they operate out of a cabin in the woods near Macon on a wildlife refuge, but hell if they are real people the could be anywhere, probably sitting right in front of me. They evolved into talking 24 hours a day 7 days a week every second of every day. Been that way for around a year and a half."

The agents looked at each other. To Shep it was a look of consideration. Thompson shrugged like "Who knows, maybe" then turned back to Shep. "Can you hear them now?"

Shep nodded, adding, "Look I know that my brain is capable of going haywire and causing all this but the way things fell into place repeatedly and matched up with the voices, more than anything has got me thinking, maybe not possible now but it want be long before you could do what it seems to be happening to me by just putting some powder nanobugs in somebody's food or drink."

The Recluses had been steady babbling bull shit trying to through Shep off his explaining. Saying things, in his ears, of a violent nature had become the norm when Shep was asked, "What are they saying now?" He knew not to say. "They just told me to kick you in the nuts then galg your eyes out." instead rewinding to what they had said an hour ago. ""Shep I got word that they are fixing to call the national guard into Twiggs county to help clean up this meth shit." Another one was saying he was in Kroger today and he saw a guy steeling some steaks and he didn't say any thing even though he wears a badge. He said the guy must have been pretty hungry and why steel Ramen noodles may as well get steaks. And this other mother fucker has been hollering some shit about this dude going to try and kick my ass because the dude thinks I been fucking his girlfriend I really don't know the dude and I ain't never met his girlfriend."

But the FBI musta' didn't care what they said or they already knew exactly what was being said by them. Shep thought to the Recluses. "It's that mind reading thing that squashes my fucking human bug theory. Damn, well, they ain't got to know about it."

Thompson had propped his elbows on the desk, griped his hands together rested his chin on his hands. The room was silent for a good 8 seconds as he stared at Shep. This is what Thompson came up with. "Look, this is a secure room. Its where we talk classified things. So if it was radio waves they should be blocked by the walls of this room. You follow me?"

Shep didn't hesitate. "That cheap door and that air duct stuck in the ceiling tells me different."

"Yea I didn't think you would buy that shit, but I had to try."

"It would probably be in like nano-hertz, shorter the wave the higher the penetration in most cases I think."

The agent relaxed. "I tell ya what I'm going to do. We're busting video poker machines in store's right now, they just keep putting more and more out there, must be worth it. In-between that and other stuff I will keep my eye's out for these human bug makers. You know, incase. Now your not going to go crazy and hurt people or yourself over this are you?"

"Naw man, this is as far as it goes."

As Shep was being shown to the door Agent Poindexter pointed out. "I hope you get you're life straight you know for what ever reason them voices are in your ears, you more than likely brought it on yourself."

"I will be the first to admit it, I been clean for a while now and hoped they would go away, I guess these things take time."

Agent Thompson added as the door was shutting behind Shep stepping into the hallway. "Just don't do nothing stupid."

Shep went home, told Tammy about it and got kicked out.

Chapter 42

Shep did buy a few more days at Tammy's till he could find a place to stay. He was with Eava dropping off some shit to her brother and his old lady when the subject came up of Shep looking for a room to rent. They liked the idea of the supplier living with them. Well, she did and it was her house, so Eava's brother went along with it.

The House belonged to Peggy 45 blond, blue eyes skinny, good looking woman. She inherited it from her parents along with a small trust fund. It was made of red brick, middle class in a middle class neighborhood on the north east side of Macon. Her boy friend, reminded Shep of gadget guy from the DEA office in looks mostly and attitude a little. His two sons 6 and 8 also lived in the house. And on most weekends Peggy's 15 year old daughter came to visit from her dads. That filled all the rooms, so Shep slept on the couch when he was there and when he slept.

He had borrowed the weed eater and the lawnmower from his dad. They lived in Hawaii so his dad was not using it. In the morning he would drop the two boys off at school, go cut 1 or 2 yards a day and spent the rest of the day selling meth and sharing it mostly with Cristal. He had a major crush on her and the only thing he got out the deal was to be around her. He wanted more, he wanted all of her.

Tiffany had dropped the child support being paid in to the state and Shep was paying her a good bit extra on a regular bases to make up for the time he fell behind. That's a mark he has not reached even till this day, but he's pretty sure he will reach it soon, and then some.

Two months gone buy everything going relatively smooth. Eava was staying over some nights giving him some love and attention. His trips to Stan's in the woods came more and more. He and Stan became good friends.

Shep didn't have anything really to do around the house he lived in, so he stayed gone all day

One morning he sat at the kitchen table smoking a cigarette drinking coffee and reading the paper. The mower and weed eater had been parked in the shed of Peggy's back yard. The help wanted section had an add for mechanically inclined, willing to travel. This was his ship, it had came in, so off to Home Depot to meet the captain of American Product Assembly. The man hired Shep on the spot and said the ship would sail in 2.5 hours. Shep had to go pack and take the truck to his parents and drop it off and unload the lawn mower. The captain was to pick him up there. The Job was to put together bathroom displays at Home Depot's. The catch was they needed a man up in Main to fill in a position and a truck and a man in Bridge Port, Connecticut. Shep was their man and the truck part. He spent the night in Atlanta that night at one of the employees residents close to the office. He kept the bug story and the half gram in his pocket to himself.

Up in the morning and off to Main with a young black man, who had no drivers license, and a new white Ford truck with the company logo on the doors. Shep also had a damn near empty meth bag in one pocket and a Sharpie permanent black marker in the other. Last but not least some Recluses in his ears saying, "DON'T do it Shep they will arest you for attempting to over through the government." and "Shep you remember the last time you had to drive in uncharted territory with us?" "Yea boy you ain't heard nothing yet….Shep, I forgot to say Shep."

Before the Human Bug War had made it to the other side of South Carolina it had infiltrated 16 bathrooms, Waffle Houses and gas stations alike. The one that took the time as he took care of his business to read the inside of the stall took this prudent information with him:

{AM crystal radios nano scale nanotechnology combine with nervous system, walking walky-talky. What's in your food?}

The young man in the passenger seat was kept in the dark on the frequent stops. He did have a problem with it, most people would complain that the trip is going to be twice as long. Shep explained he had to drink a lot of coffee to stay awake and he had a weak bladder so it was just going to be a long ride. Shep stopped at 25 more before he reached Maine at sunrise. He had been driving 20 hours and that was the 3rd consecutive night he had not laid down, other than a hour one night and two another. He was beat, the voices the driving the drug, he had not thought this mission totally out. In hind site, he would not have attempted it due to the level of unsafe it projected on others going down the roads. He took a three hour power nap at the motel room in Maine, and that should do it. Hell Connecticut was just right there… some where.

It only took 24 hours to make it to his second destination. 24 hours and 5 trips across the Washington bridge seeing the Empire State Building and empty space that was the World Trade Center, China town 2 time, ventured out toward the Hampton's, found Queens, unsuccessful at taking naps in truck, burning 4 hours in Baskin Robins parking lot but did write on the stall there, second time at a picnic area on the Hudson river. Wrote on some walls in Salem, Massachusetts. Saw nothing with Connecticut on it, saw a sign pointing to Woodstock, but just didn't have it in him. New Jersey turn pike took him bout all night, and put him a state or two below his destination but hey it was much easier to get there from the bottom up. Shep can read maps. He has a good sense of direction. I was just having a bad day.

On his way back across Virginia he stopped at a small gas station, near some signs reading the CIA head quarters close by. Luckily his creative genius had not been hampered by his abuse. He had parked around the side his truck unable to be seen from the inside. Tearing the back page off the truck owners manual, it was blank, he put his plan into action.

The mom and pop store was exactly what Shep was hoping for. The Lady of 65ish in her straw garden hat was not named Patel, probably Smith or Jones. The pic on the wall of her and most likely her husband looked American. The empty store would soon have customers from the gas pump so Shep seized the moment. Being really in a hurry added to the drama.

Walking noticeably fast around the store Shep stepped to the counter with a Coke he looked her in her eyes and slid the folded up paper toward her and nodded at it. Then noticed a look of worry on her face, maybe thinking it was a stick up. Maybe she had saw it on T.V. too. Still not sure why they use the note, unless using the drive thru.

He cleared it up. "Mam, I have been involved with classified work for the CIA. What they are doing just ain't right, so I stole some technology from the lab that needs to be shown to some big wigs over at the Department of Human Rights. The CIA are on my heals looking for me. I was supposed to meet a partner here with in the next 48 hours. I can't get in touch with him. He was going to call and advise me on the time. He always has a yellow tie on he has black hair about my height. Just give this to the next one in here with a yellow tie fitting that script. I'll have to take my chances, I got to get out of this town." He tapped the note with his fingers and asked how much for the Coke.

Her look, what ever it was, was a bit more pronounced than when Shep got to the counter. It slowly faded to a smile that matched her Hill Billy draw. "I sure will, and the cokes on the house."

Other customers made it to the counter as Shep took back up his brisk walk, leaving the store with an announcement. "This country will not fall under your watch mamm, thank you!"

The note:

{I have some AM radio nano transceivers, they are not mixed with the nerve combining agent, but I have it also. They have experiments on going in the public sector. I also have a crucial part of the base station. Can't stay to hot. Stay at your local I will get back with you}

Standing ovation from the Recluses.

Chapter 43

Shep was nodding and swerving his way in to Bridge Port. MacDonald's then after that finally the room. Them voices just kept on and on.

Inside waiting for his order to be filled a set of three took their place to order. A child, a older lady and there she was like double cherry pie, like disco super-fly. The three inch heels supported white leather knee high boots, the tight jeans tucked in them held thick thighs to a well rounded body covered with a loose fitting pink and white tie-die shirt, her spiraling tight curly hair draped over her shoulders, and her green eye's had lights behind them that made them glow.

He tried not to stare but just looked like he was watching a tennis match. He noticed she was staring at him so he manned up and spoke. "What's up, I need to know where the Budget Inn is."

She spoke with a thick Port Rican accent. "When you leave out this way," She pointed "go down three stop lights, it will be there."

One of the agents pointed out. "Where was she three thousand miles ago, Shep? Coulda' saved you a few days." The others had steady been trying to through him off his game. They jumped on that wagon. Shep jumped on it to, but kept his better attention turned to her.

"I just got here from Georgia."

She interrupted him. "When you talk I like." That's what her grin was saying too.

"I don't thank I'll be here long, but as long as I am, what's a man do for fun around here."

"You can come see me. Five o clock, I work at, Keystone." She pointed. "It is two stop lights that way take a right."

Shep picked his to go bag up and with a tad bit of extra enthusiasm gave his opinion on her plan. "That sounds like a great idea, see you later."

"K, I looking for you."

Upon arriving at the motel Shep met his two working partners. One was older than Shep and the other was younger. The older one seemed distraught or maybe constipated and talked like a Yankee. "Where have you been? We expected you last night."

"I been every where twice, long ride."

The room had two beds and a cot with a mattress on it for Shep. He sat on it, no problem. After he ate and took a shower he made use of the cot. Waking up several hours later to the low sound of the TV and the two coworkers almost whispering as not to bother him. It took about 20 seconds for the agents at he cabin to get back inside. Ten of them, including Tiffina and Scooter had gathered around a fire and had some hot dogs and hamburgers on the grill. Scooters treat. They had left the mic unattended since Shep was out of it. The Bluetooth that one of them had on his ear alerted him with Shep's thoughts, but he was in the middle of fixing his plate so he finished what he was doing before going inside the cabin and telling Shep what Shep just told you.

He got off the cot, check the time, 6:00pm, put on some jeans, pulled a flannel button down and t-shirt out of his bag. "I met this bad ass chic at Micky Dees, she wants me to come see her tonight at the Keystone. y'all know where that is?"

The younger gave directions. "One light that way and take a right, we rode by it a few times. I think it's a bar."

The voice. "Shep you learn fast don't you, just ask man you will get there a lot faster." A few more had started joining in as they finished eating.

Shep addressed the two coworkers. "y'all want to go?" "He was picking up the keys and headed for the door.

He got unanimous participation from the Recluses, with Tiffina adding. "Damn rite I'm going, just too make sure you behave yourself."

The young dude declined. The older one questioned the whole adventure. "You think that's a good idea? We need to be at Home Depot at eleven, got a lot of work to do tonight. We already behind for waiting on the truck to get here, and you been driving for two days. Don't you need some sleep?"

"Be time enough to sleep when I'm dead."

Shep scoped the, dim, smoky, room, it had a oval bar in the center surrounded by mostly old men looking like sea farers. The bartender was not young but had no problem showing her cleavage in a cut up black t-shirt and Daisy Dukes. He bought a beer, collected the last 18 dollars change he had to his name, looked around and there she was, double cherry pie. In a thong bikini. Mind you it was 40 degrees out side.

Next thing Shep knew she had took him by the hand, led him to a small room with mirrors covering the walls and ceiling, planted him in a barber chair in the center, let the back of it half way down and spoke the first words said since she spoke to him at the hamburger joint, as she straddled his legs with her knees in the chair. The accent sexy. "You so mmm, mmm, mmm, I want you."

Shep put his hand on her waste and she put them back on the arm rest. He got the point. She started grinding on his lap in super slow motion, looking in his eyes. She flexed her tongue at him.

Shep praised her. "You so fucking hot."

She took her top off and rubbed her firm titts hard. Grinding harder on his lap, suddenly springing off him and dropping her tongs to the floor, grabbing his belt like it had to be loosened immediately. His pants were on the floor his cock pulled out the front of his boxers, her lips, not the ones she ran that sexy talk out of, the other ones, grinded without penetration. They both pushed harder and harder and she got more vocal as the thick wetness was felt coming from her down below, her arms around his neck, she started whispering in his ear. "I want to take you home, you talk to me and fuck me, please."

You would think they would give a ol' boy a break, but no, they was in his ear the entire time yelling for him to give them his attention not her. He couldn't ignore them so he multi-tasked.

She turn loose and went insane on his lap clawing at his chest, she soaked him with her thickness, suddenly dropping between his legs, her knees on the floor she grabbed him tight and finished him off."

Tiffina's voice "Damn Shep I'm the jealous one now…..Scooter giving me the evil eye now." Others just kept up the B.S.

The two sex perv's got their attire in order. She hinted "I don't know if you pay me or I pay you. Shep emptied his wallet. They had some small talk that led to her asking. "I need a man around the house, you come stay with me?"

Shep declined on account he was penniless and for that reason it didn't seem right. He said this instead, "I work for the CIA, you know the CIA?

"Federollys"

"That's the ones. They hired me down in Georgia to help them hunt down some of their own, that stole some technology from their laboratory. It's communication technology, that is nanotechnology."

"Nano?"

"Very tiny, anyway they put this shit in some folks I know that operate methamphetamine labs, now the rouge Feds are on radios talking to the meth lab folks and the meth lab folks hear them in their ears. I know because they talk to me in my ears. That's why they brought me along, in hopes I will hear some clue on where they are running to. I don't really do anything. The ones I'm with use this scanner and a computer to locate them, and we go after them but they always gone before we get there, and they been careful not to give me any clue but never stop talking. We should have another location in a few hours and I will be moving on."

"They talk to you?"

"Yea."

Scooter gave Shep one of them slow claps that gets faster then everybody joins in. After that they started asking him about that disease he just got from her and how he was going to make it all night at work with no meth. On and on and on.

She took his hand and they made good by's. He got back to the motel with a few hours to rest. He got through the night, and the next, but not with out telling the coworkers the true story of the nano bug experience. That led to a phone call to the boss in Atlanta. Shep was in the shower and when he came out the bathroom he was handed the phone. The boss said thanks' for everything, he was buying a bus ticket and Shep would be going back to Macon and receive a check for his hours in the mail.

Shep ain't asked why, who, or what. He let the boss know he appreciated the job and told him he hoped everything worked out for him. Grey Hound was a long rout but not near as long as the one Shep took. He wrote on some Grey Hound bus station's bathroom stall's during the 4 lay over's. Glad to be going home and going home with another chapter in the human bug experience.

Chapter 44

Shep was sitting in his truck after pulling up the hill and coasting backwards into Peggy's driveway. He was returning from Stan's with some meth.

Thinking "Yea, Yea, Yea, Yea, Shep, Shep, Shep, Shep it's been around three years since y'all started talking non stop and I hate my name."

Voice, "Yea Shep it's Bugology Shep." Shep heard a car door shut in his ear, then Tiffina's voice "Shep I am leaving my parents house headed for my place just thought I would check in on you…Shep….Yea." "Shep you stupid fuck why in the hell are we still talking to you, and why dose she get a bug phone and we still have to come to the cabin." Scooter's voice came in. "Because I gave her a bug phone, Shep I am in California walking down Sunset Strip." "Yea Shep this is CIA agent Martin, I am in Virginia and I pulled rank and got me a bug phone." They just always talked and hollered.

Shep said out loud as he got out his truck, "Reckon that makes me nationwide don't it."

Shep found Peggy and her boyfriend sitting on the couch watching TV. The two boys were in the back yard playing.

Shep informed them. "I got it."

Peggy handed him a foil already folded with a straw. He pulled out the bag. "I went by my aunt's on the way back and got some mail. Looks like I will be going to court in two weeks for felony obstruction of an officer and terrorist threat of a federal agent.

The boy friend said alarmingly, "Terrorist threat on a federal agent?"

He had not told them about that. "What happen was......." He gave them the story ending with, he thought it was dropped because it had not came back up and it was so long ago.

He went to the law library at the Bibb County court house and did some research. Self defense law said he could use necessary force to defend himself if there was reasonable belief he was in danger and necessary force being words or action. It also said that if he claimed it there is a shift of burden and he dose not have to prove his innocents they have to prove him guilty. So if since he reasonably believed that Sterling had some control over the voices, he had every right to try and stop them with a terrorist threat. The proof that he believed, the voices were real was the fact he made the call. Just like if a cop shoots somebody thinking they have a gun and so the cop shoots first finding no gun on the other he is protected as long as the court can't show there was not just cause. In Shep's case the court would have to prove he was not a human bug. They couldn't prove that for the lack of technology and incase he was it would be a threat to national security so ground for acquittal.

Shep sat on the bench that reminded him of a church pew in the hall way area outside the court room. The tall, thin, lawyer wore a not so formal suit his chiseled face showed no hint of a good day, and his gray hair showed he had been around this rodeo for a while. He told Shep to follow him to an office.

The paisley carpet complemented the stained wood office walls and book shelves. The lawyer sat half ass on the wood desk and Shep slid his chair back and took a seat. "Mr. Shep I have gotten you a deal from the DA. I had to do some talking but he went for it. It's a five year suspended sentence, meaning your going to be on probation for five years."

Shep threw manners to the wind. "Bull Shit I ain't guilty. When I told you what had happen you said don't worry about it that officer had a history of this sort of thing, open and shut case."

The lawyer boosted his tail feathers. "Now you know you were over there at your ex-wife's causing problems and now your going to pay the price and take this plea and the officer statement says you tried to pull a knife on him and you was high on drugs."

"No Hell I did not either. Did you get the camera footage from the car, it shows the Sheriffs son cussing the Deputy out for attacking me."

"The camera was not working."

"Well ain't that just damn convenient. Look man I ain't guilty."

"Then we just going to say your guilty." He stood from the desk and went out the door.

Shep was on his heals. "No we are not."

And low and behold who was standing in the hallway a few doors down leaning his back against the wall but the Sheriff's son. The Lawyer wasted no time in proving his case. "Detective on the day Mr. Shep was at his ex-wife's did he provoke that arrest."

The Detective stared at the floor "Mr. Shep should have put his hands where the officer could see them."

The Lawyer looked at Shep and with out saying a word Shep knew he was resting his case.

Shep knew they had him with lies but they had him and showing his ass right then and there would only get him locked up. He asked if he had time to go smoke before court started. The Detective said go ahead. The Lawyer added, "Don't run off or there will be a bench warrant issued."

Shep sat in the court session till lunch and it was over he was to return the next day. Hind site is 20/20, he should have went back the next day and agreed with that lawyer with humbleness pouring from his eyes. Then when he stood before that judge and the judge asked if he had any thing he wanted to say, he should have gave him the truth about this whole situation, and spoke the truth with great assertiveness. That ain't what happened at all, not at all.

Chapter 45

Rather than show up for court and let the Jones County mob send him swinging from the gallows pole he spent that Friday doing what he normally would do hustling what he had left and buying cold pills to go to Stan's and cook them down. He had no idea what to do about the bench warrant. He hoped it would all some how magically disappear.

Come Saturday morning Shep was coasting backwards down the hill into Peggy's driveway. He was listening to the scolding of the new shift in his ears. The shift of the night before had a night of projecting voices in to the woods all around Shep and Stan as they did the dirty deed of mixing and filtering. Shep kept his cool in the woods he knew if it was some Po Po out there, him and Stan could do nothing about it but take what they had coming.

You would think with all this meth Shep would be able to hire the best lawyer in town instead of getting stuck with this cracker jack that had an office beside the court house. Not the case at all, after he took care of Tiffany with child support, giving catch up extra, and gas in the old truck, insurance, paid his rent with meth, shared with Cristal, Tammy, Eava, and did a lot of it himself, he just did make it to the next cook.

After freshening up with a shower and change of cloths and brushing his teeth. That brushing his teeth he did often with the tooth brush and mouth wash he kept in the glove compartment of the truck, being that the meth addiction seemed to give rot mouth. He eventually made it to Tammy's and spent Saturday night knocking boots with her and watching her run around the trailer in her panties ripping everything out the closets and throwing it all back in. He found a vitamin bottle from one of the closets and it had gel caps in it. Breaking the caps apart he emptied the content out and filled up 20 caps with a half gram each of meth.

When he got to Peggy's just before lunch the next day, her boyfriend met him at the door with the Sunday Macon Telegraph. Shep's pic in the crime stoppers section was a good looking, sexy one and that's all the good he saw in it. He had price on his head. The voices had been saying he was in for a big suprize but they were always saying not necessarily that exactly but stuff like that, still it almost made them into being real people. One of them started singing off key, "Shep it's like Bon Jovi said man, "*I'm wanted dead or alive, I walk these streets six string on.........*"" The rest of them joined in with Tiffina's voice telling them to stop, stop, she was sitting at home on the toilet and they were ruining her dump.

He could not have the U.S. Marshalls kicking in his friends doors looking for him. So he had to turn himself in. What the hell was thinking missing court anyway. Figuring he would get a good meal from his aunt (Mama Jean) Deryl's mama, before he went to eat his food off jail house trays, and tell the family he was on the way to give himself up he got cleaned up and headed for Gailu. Dr.

For better insight Google map the street in satellite view. Shep turned on the street and normally he would go to the turn around and come back the beginning of the street to Mama Jean's and park on the side of the road, no reverse to back out the driveway.

Not today, because his pic was in crime stoppers and of all days Sterling and the rest of his family could be seen out in his moms yard at the turn around end of the street. Quick thinking Shep whipped into the first driveway on the right. His grand mama's (MaMo) driveway. It is a horse shoe that circles back around to Hwy. 80. He pulled over to the shop with out blocking himself in. Deryl's van was parked there and some cars he did not recognize. The lights being on he knocked on the locked door of the shop.

Deryl opened the door. "You need to go turn yourself in" and slammed the door.

The voices stopped whatever they had been saying and went with. "FUUUUUCK THAT SHIT, Shep kick that door in and give that stupid fuck what for!" Sterling's voice in a whisper. "Shep I am in my mama's bathroom so I can talk to you and piss. Take your ass over there and tell Doyle and Mama Jean to take you to Jones County LEC."

Shep was already walking two doors down to Mama Jeans. Thinking "I am going to eat and go to David and Carlines to have them take me to Jones County, I got to go see Tammy first and fuck." Sterling had no Bluetooth on and had cut his bug phone off anyway so he did not hear that part.

While Shep was in his aunt's eating, she had made the chicken fajitas Shep would die for, things took place outside on Gailu. Dr that would make the day interesting to say the least.

A Bibb County Sherriff Deputy, in rout east on Hwy. 80 had been seen by Sterling's brother Sonny. The same Sonny Shep had worked with and smoked meth with in the geneses of it all. The Bibb Deputy had to drop a inmate off at the Dry Branch post office 100 yards past Gailu dr. to a Twiggs Deputy.

Sonny and his wife saw an opportunity to get some reward money for turning Shep in and made their way to the post office to give a lead on his capture. The Twiggs Deputy got the inmate, the Bibb Deputy got the info on Shep's local and Sonny got his name on the list for reward money.

Shep bid his good byes to his family, a stop by Tammy's in mind then off to his friends that did not do meth to have them take him in. It would be a good place to leave his truck and gave him the opportunity to spend the time with Tammy.

Shep pulled out his MaMo's drive way going toward Twigg's County just in time to see the Twiggs Deputy turn out the post office heading in the same direction as he. The Bibb Deputy came toward Shep. They met on Hwy. 80 in slow motion eye to eye. The Deputy, black hair, thick mustache, stout in statue. The next thing he noticed was the vitamin bottle laying in the seat by his leather jacket. He put his jacket over it and eased on the gas.

The Deputy turned in MaMo's driveway and parked at the shop, while radioing in to Twiggs to get permission to be in hot pursuit of Shep.

Deryl saw the Deputy from with in the shop through the roll up door windows and in order to protect the poached deer they had hanging from the rafters with out a tag on it, he went out to see the matter. He confirmed it being Shep so the Deputy would not have a look around.

Shep was pouring on the throttle, turning off 80 in the direction of his friends. He went by Tammy's driveway rubber necking but stopping was not an option anymore. The Twiggs Deputy had continued on down 80 with the inmate headed for the jail so he was not an issue. Shep laid on the gas straightening some curves and flattened some hills. To the Recluses egging it on in every way imaginable. Of course the news spread and the ones with the bug phones had all tuned in, Tiffina, Blair the FBI agent, Martin CIA and Sterling had done left his mamas to sit up at the store and listen in. Scooter was God only knows where singing the Dukes of Hazard theme.

Shep steady checking the road in his wake. He saw nothing. Reaching a cross roads, his next turn, on a blind hill, he slowed no stop sign in his direction and took a left. On that corner to his left is an old cement block store long ago abandoned grown over with vines and a grassy area to the other side of it. He was on a straight away a mile and a quarter long, nothing behind him, nothing, nothing. Son of a bitch, Bibb County in hot pursuit on a Twiggs County back road. The Deputy car was about two feet off his bumper and had no lights flashing or sirens on. The truck was traveling at 55 in a 45. This continued around a curve and half way down a hill when Shep put on his left blinker and turned into his friends driveway. Up a gravel hill around a circle, bringing the new double wide into sight and the new tan Chevy truck and blue Grand Marquis. Shep turned kin the direction he had came from and pointed himself back out the driveway and put it in park rolling down his window. The Deputy came from his car in a rush, He could be seen from Shep's large side view mirror. "PUT YOUR HANDS where I can see them, NOW!"

That made Shep's balls burn for some reason and he did not liker the site of the Deputy coming at him fast reaching Shep's back tire by that point with his Billy club in hand, positioned to put a good lick on his head.

Just some good ol' boys never meaning no harm. Shep punched the gas snatching the truck down to drive. Gravel binged the front of the car and a pebble or two may have hit the Deputy. Shep didn't stop to find out, he took the chase back out the driveway stopping to reflect on how much shit he was in now before turning onto the road in the direction he had came from with no destination in mind.

The car now had blue lights blazing and siren wailing. Up the hill at 40 mph. Voices tripping "You just a regular fucking OJ and you Shep." Tiffina's voice "SHEP WHAT THE HELL YOU DO THT FOR?"

Into the curve before the straight away Buddy long (Cool old cat) in his home made snatch truck was wondering why Shep was behind him with sirens in his truck, the cop was too close to Shep's bumper for buddy to see it in his rear view. It finally got the picture and pulled off the side of the road letting Shep with his slow speed chase go on by at speeds of 45 mph.

The straight away presented it's own problems, considering the Twiggs Deputy up ahead, closer to the vines growing over the old store.

He was turning his car T-Bone across the road, with plenty of room to go around on both sides the road. Shep got closer and Deputy Spokes, who Shep was familiar with from having the same friends back in high school days, had drawn his pistol and set the sights between Shep's eye's. The car behind him was not backing off.

Shep got close enough to see the inmate still in the back of Spokes's car. He could not help a smile thinking the inmate wanted to see his brains be blown out the back window of the truck so there was no way he was coming unglued from the window even if he was fixing to kiss the front of a 73' Chevy truck.

Around 200 feet from the pistol between his eye's he eased the truck off to his passenger side of the road and window still down watched Spokes holster his weapon as the truck went by at 15 mph on the shoulder.

Spokes asked as if Shep was sticking his finger in some dog shit, "Shep what are you doing?"

"I don't know man."

In the short distance to the stop sign he had two Po Po's on his ass. The blind hill from the left the entrance road to Dry Branch Kaolin in front of him and from where he had came a over grown store with a grass field beside it. The Bibb car shot around him and into the road, if a car had been coming at the usual 60 mph up that hill Shep would be looking at man slaughter charges. Enough was enough Shep turned into the store and across the parking lot to the field did a spin out 180 and fish tailed a few times coming to rest looking at Spokes with his pistol in hands pointed at the ground smiling and shaking his head. Seeing Shep get out the truck with his hand raised.

Spokes ordered, "On the ground man, on the ground!"

Shep fell to his knees and put his hands behind him.

"All the way flat on the ground!"

Shep thought suicide by cop, all he had to do was bring his pistol finger around real fast and he would be done with the voices and all. Tiffina, "Shep you know better than that."

He fell to his belly and Spokes was clicking the cuffs as Shep explained, "Man Jones County are trying to lock me up for protecting the ones I love it is a self defense law and they attacked me and pepper SPRAYD ME FOR DOING THE RIGHT THING!"

By this time the Bibb deputy had parked got his shotgun out the trunk and when Spokes got off his back the Bibb Deputy took the shot gun stock pointed down barrel in hands like post hole diggers and with all he had drove the stock down into Shep's lower back just to the side of his spinal colum. Once twice three times.

Spokes grabbed the gun. "HEY, HEY, he's cuffed, he's cuffed."

"Son of a bitch through rocks all over me."

Shep was picked up grass and dirt on his shirt and face, to see Sterling sitting in his truck in the store parking lot, with Sonny and his wife in there car and Buddy long and some passer by he did not know. The blow from the shot gun kicked in and his right side went out and he dropped like a sack of taters to the ground."

The Bibb Deputy put him in the back of his car after Spokes told him he did not want him. Shep protested in the back of the car. "y'all are going to hand me over to these mother fuckerss! They are lying about everything in the court the lost the camera footage and y'all muther fuckers are going to hand me OVER TO THEM!

Spokes had the truck door open and lifted the jacket up finding the vitamin bottle. Shep Bluetooth to the aw' stricken Recluses. "Looks like I fixing to get my first ever drug charge." Spokes looked in the bottle shook the 18 half grams it around and gave the other cop a look shook it around and put the cap on it and put it back under the jacket. Shep did not say another word. He was booked in Bibb County for eluding, obstruction, damage to government property.

Chapter 46

A voice "Shep how much more can you take of this, a 6x9 cell, stuck in it twenty hours a day, only to go in that dayroom and it ain't no better there. The loud ass inmates hollering from cell to cell, us fucking with you every second your awake, twenty-two hours a day, and starving you to death, Shep you ate the chicken bones on your tray the other day, how much more?"

"If my dad and all them other's could handle Vietnam I can handle this." It was thinking like that that got him to the next few minutes, but the thought of death seemed so nice, he wanted death. He had not the guts to do it.

Tiffina was sitting on the back porch at her parents house alone, waiting on her mom to finish making taco's and her dad was in his recliner asleep in the den. Shep knew this because she had told him just five minutes before. "Shep you hang in there and I will give you a good treat tonight when I get home and go to bed."

"You going to talk sexy dirty to me again, I love it when you do that."

Dumbass's voice. "She will do no such thing Shep! Shep I am getting out my car going into Wall-Mart and when I get back I am going toooooo…."

Shep finished the sentence. "Go home?" It was uncontrollable.

Tiffina tapped in. "Shep time for me to eat, but like I pointed out the other day, he is at the cabin and pissed off because Scooter won't give him a bug phone. Scooter is out recruiting us some relief cause we had a lot of MIB's move on and when that relief gets here I will be gone for a while so tonight is the last time you will hear me for a little while."

Dumbass's voice. "What the fuck ever. Shep I am going toooo…."

"Make it quiet in here?"

"No, Shep I am going toooo….."

"Mama's?"

"No, Shep I am going toooo….."

Dumbass had 20 minutes on left the mic and left it on repeat the entire time.

He had been on the Bibb County LEC block for a month up to this point. A month later when he got his day in court it was a great day. The court appointed lawyer was a young man and very nice and helpful. He surprised Shep. "I got your charges dropped to a reckless driving and that carries 700 dollars in fines and a year probation."

Shep said. "Run it."

That evening he was picked up by Jones County from Bibb LEC and taken the Jones LEC. The two months there went a little better than the last. Jones County had good food and he was in a cell pod. A big open area with tables and a TV surrounded with two levels of cell's up stairs and down stairs, 4 men to a cell. Locked in them only at night during bed time. He told the Human bug experience so many times he got tired of telling it. But his fellow inmates liked the story and would encourage him to tell it to the next one that had not heard it.

The voices kept up the talking with new voices coming in but not all the old ones left. Shep could tell the change, it was kinda neat hearing the new ones settle in with a lot of, "This is what ya'll been doing for how long?" "So I am I doing this right, I mean what the hell I am I supposed to talk about?" "I came from a Marine boot camp and boy you got it bad, AND THAT IS WHAT I DO, FUCK YOU IN THE SKULL BOY!" Another voice tells him. "You forgot to say Shep, always start with Shep." "I say that every time I start?" "Yea, and say Yea a lot." "Yea?" "Yea" "SHEP! YEA!" "Close enough man keep going."

Two month's and he was in the holding cell at the Jones County court house. Last on the docket for some reason. He was called out to the hallway to meet with that chiseled face cracker jack lawyer and it was no better than the last time.

Standing in the hall the lawyer asked. "So you ready to take this plea?"

"What if I want to go to trial with it. How long will that take?"

"Six months maybe longer."

"Run the plea, and I get out to day?"

"Today."

"Lets do it."

Shep got out and picked his truck up from a friends who had got it out the impound for him. Went to Peggy's to be greeted by her boyfriend who opened the front door with. "You can't live here any more your shits in the shed in the back yard" and slammed the door.

Shep saw no point in taking that any further so he got his shit and sold a few caps on down the road. Then to his Mama Jean's to eat and was told he could stay there for a week and he better find job. He did the next day in Warner Robins doing residential electrical work. The second day on his way home the transmission went out on the truck. He got Ben, Deryl's other brother to help him tow it to the shop in MaMo's yard.

The next day he had his things packed and after work had a coworker drop him off at a motel room in Warner Robins. He kept working and the meth ran out, he was stuck living paycheck to paycheck. The room was lonely all his friends too far away to get him, figuring the time away and work would do him good. The voices, not good company. He told anybody who would listen the human bug experience. It did not get him fired the boss liked it.

He was in a never ending bind at the motel just making enough to cover the room and eat. When he struck up a conversation with a man at near by gas station that needed help doing remodeling jobs. He would pay Shep two more dollars an hour than he then made. Shep quit the electrical job and took the new job. Son of a bitch picked him up the first week and paid him. The next week his new boss only picked him up three days and paid him and told him he didn't have enough to do.

Shep had to leave Warner Robins there was just no chance for him there anymore. And he had to get back closer to the meth. The voices had him down to pure misery.

He had Deryl's daddy come pick him up and take him back to Macon where he took the money he had left and got a super cheep motel room in down town Macon. He was walking the mile away walk to the Salvation Army to eat the free meal served for supper, with not two nickels to rub together, when he came across and elderly man pushing a pallet jack with a big bundle of folded up tarps on it. Shep gave him a hand pushing the stubborn jack up into the building.

"You need a job?"

"Yes sir. I was just walking up to the salvation army to eat, truck broke down, lost my job, got a room just down on Riverside dr. I can start in the morning. The man pulled out his wallet gave Shep a ten and said be here at 7:30 we put up tents for weddings and other events and we have to be on the mark so don't be late."

Turned out to be some of the nicest, best people you would ever want to meet at Macon Tent Rentals. In the month and a half that followed, Shep had got Stan to pick him up a few times to get right with the meth. The motel was still lonely though. He did not trust the riff raff that hung around it so kept to himself.

After work one night he had worked late he went to the room and freshened up then set out on a walk to the Waffle House with his voices still going nonstop. Wearing a tank top and shorts, tennis shoes, only two blocks away at 10pm. The sound of a car stopping next to the empty curb behind him and from the sound of clap, clap, clap shoes that followed him he new the not reporting to the Jones County probation office had just caught up with him.

"Excuse me, sir Excuse me do you have some ID?"

Locked on the block in Bibb County for two days waiting for Jones County. A month in Jones County and his day in court for revocation of his probation. Shep got in front of that judge with out a lawyer and told him "What had happened was….." And with protest from the probation officer the DA shot her down and sided with Shep and so did the judge.

Judge said. "Mr. Shep I am putting you on non report status and you owe us not a dime, you stay out of trouble and you will not hear from us again, you are free to go."

Shep went to his Mama Jeans again, who had got his belongings from the motel. She told Shep that if will behave he could stay in MaMo's house, she had moved in with them on account of her old timers, but she wanted the rent and bills paid so he best have a job.

"OK" He called Stan and Stan picked him up on his way to heist some anhydrous ammonia from that place in Atlanta. Stan looked out for him after all was said and done he paid Shep enough cash and meth to get a used transmission for his truck and enough left over to get back on track.

Shep bought some cans of spray paint while working on getting the new transmission in. He painted the truck solid primer gray then took a flat black, going around the truck in erratic lines then a glossy black light mist over that. Dusk till Dawn Camouflage he called it.

AND THEM RECLUSES JUST KEPT ON AND ON AND ON

Chapter 47

Shep settled in to his grand mama's. He was looking for a job, not whole heartedly. The days had been comfortable. That was heating up quick. Shep had to move out of the house it was not a permanent fix. Mama Jean was on him about saving money to get his own place. She decided she would help him save some money.

The red brick house on the east corner of Hwy. 80 and Gailu dr. was built with a living area consisting of a bedroom, kitchen and living room. A door led to a hallway with two bedrooms and living area. The area with the kitchen had its own central air, and full bath as did the hallway section.

Mama Jean sent Uncle Doyle to disconnect the A/C unit for the hallway section and that's the location of the bedroom Shep used.

He showered daily and kept the sheets and such washed so the odd smell that had came to be in his bed room one morning raised questions. Still laying in the bed he thought about it. "The temp is fairly warm, but why the smell. It is a smell of musky, but with a twang."

Sterling's voice had been telling him to get his ass up out the bed for the last 10 min. He reminded Shep of the 4x6 foot safe Shep was wondering about the other day in the bedroom closet. "Shep, I did not have time to tell you this story the other day, I had stuff to do."

"Well, when ever your ready, time to listen to y'all is what I do."

"You know my dad and your granddad were friends. This is what he told my daddy and my daddy told me this story when I was in first grade and a real big bully was picking on me."

"Shep it goes like this, You know your Granddaddy Hortman was no stranger to the colored folks, as he would say, because as a young teen growing up in Phoenix City Alabama he ran moonshine all down through the quarters. Even not being all that big in statute it did not scare him, because he knew how to deal with people. SO, when he moved to Dry Branch and was building that house your in back in 1962 he went down to Black Bottom rd. right there in Twiggs County and hired some "colored" men to do the framing and got him an old brick mason down that way named Jewels."

"On this morning your Granddaddy's brother Phillip was talking to the framers up on the floor decking as they put the walls up. Their brother Bill was messing with that safe in that closet there. Being to big to get in after the doors had been framed. Like you said it has a combination and a key lock, air tight, water proof, fire proof. Granddaddy Hortman was standing up on the decking going over a few things with the brick man."

Shep noticed Sterling had everybody's attention. This was to be the longest one voice talk Shep had heard in a little over three years.

"A fifties model pick up truck came from the west on 80. A little older than middle aged white man was just a looking on his way by. The truck did a 180 and came back to the driveway, pulling up to the house and somebody must have pissed in his Cheerios that morning."

He got out the truck and went right up on the decking. "Who owns this property?"

Granddaddy Hortman looked at him sideways. "That is me Walter Hortman."

The man grunted and looked around. "Why are you hiring all these niggers? We got white folks that need jobs."

"It's my property, I expect I hire who I want to hire."

Now this man ran so deep with his hate he couldn't see out the hole he was in. "Mr. Hortman, have you ever heard of the Klu Klux Klan?"

"I reckon so."

"We got ways of putting vice on those that stray."

Granddaddy Hortman lost his temper with the threat from the stranger. "Mister I'll take care of you right now."

The Klan's man jolted a few times saying. "I'm shaking in my boots."

Granddaddy Hortman kept what is known as a flapjack, as well as other names, in his back pocket. Shep knew what it was, he had seen his Granddaddy with one and Uncle Phillip. A leather strap about ten inches long, a half inch thick, shaped like a tennis racket with a very wide handle. The big end is loaded with lead and with the right flick of the wrist that lead could shatter a skull.

Any way the man said he was "shaking in his boots".

Granddaddy Hortman was quicker than greased rattle snake with that flapjack and informed the man of his intentions. "I'll put you in a safe place then." The man felt the lead to his head and lost what little since he had. The safe was wide open. "Put him in that safe Bill." Bill and Phillip grabbed the all but falling on the floor body and shoved him in the safe. What little protest he had was no match for the two Hortmans'. He was going in that safe.

Bill kicked the door shut barely missing Phillips hand. They all sat around and laughed about it for a minute. Granddaddy had no intention on killing the man. He was just sending a message that if they wanted to play dirty he was more than ready. "I thank he done learned his lesson Bill let him out."

It was the first Bill had thought that far ahead. "Walter, I opened that safe and when this idiot came up here with all that mess I laid the key and the paper with the combination on it down in the safe, we ain't going to get him out alive."

"GREAT TIME'a DAY." Granddaddy took a few steps in all directions.

Jewls put in his. "Mr. Hortman you bets get rid of that safe, or it goona bring you worlds of trouble."

Getting rid of the safe would bother Granddaddy. He had paid a good bit of money for it and just couldn't let it go, no matter if he couldn't use it again. "Bill get in that mans truck and follow me." Bill followed him to a chalk mine hole that they had dug chalk out of for so long they was hauling the chalk out of China. Nothing left after that so they let it fill up with water. Say that truck ain't hit bottom yet.

Sterling informed Shep on that smell. "That's what you smelling man, as it get hotter in that room, he starts fermenting like wine. The pressure is released but air can't get back in, So you smelling MUSKY-KLAN-WINE!"

Shep gave the Bluetooth's his thinking, "Awesome story and if Sterling, well Sterling's voice, his personality in my head, that personality just took my memories of Granddaddy saying the phrase "Somebody needs to put him in a safe place." and he said it a hand full of times I was witness to. I never knew how he came to say it. That personality took that and concocted this story with my mind having no idea what he was leading too. That's what y'all have been doing all along. I've known that, but this is just it at its best. My sub mind able to plan elaborate things with me having no idea it's doing so."

Voices "YEA Shep real fucking deep!" "Shep what it all boils down to is you're a God Damn human bug." "Shep, by the way great story Sterling, I like it when you go off on them crazy trains, gives me something to listen to besides the same shit we done said."……………on and on

Chapter 48

Bill Gates was in the federal court house in Washington D.C.. Microsoft monopolizing the market had become a issue with Apple Computer and others. This was being covered by CNN and other news net works on the hour. Shep had a great idea.

It was about 9 pm when he called 411 info and asked for the law offices of Microsoft in Washington D.C.. He called the number he received. A recording gave him the option of several attorneys' extensions. He chose the first one. A recording then said to leave a message.

"My name is Shep and I am going to give it to you straight up. This originated with meth labs in Dry Branch, Georgia. This is true, a CIA and FBI agent was down from D.C. doing a job background check and a friend of mine and the DEA had eyes on the house I lived in, when I started hearing voices in my ears not my head. They said they were renegade cops. I am not lying they said things were going on other than where I was at and most of it, pretty much all of it was bullshit, BUT if I look at the laws of probability they got it right too many times or close to right." (The truth is they got the stories close to right about the same amount a fortune teller

would when he says "You have a person close to you that is very sick?"
Shep was trying to save the world so he didn't tell it like that to them.)

"Nanotechnology, AM crystal radios on a nano scale with a constituent that combines with the nervous system, nano hertz. Man, just put in food, a billion plus, and when ate, you have a human bug. Lets see, oh maybe reverse effect with sending vibrations of crystals from sound, like they generate electricity from rapid vibration, anyway you get the point. Why talk to me, it was human nature, to experiment on different levels. Thank you."

He called back and left a similar message on another extension. He did not expect the world to suddenly end as we know it. He did not expect to hear anything about it, not from Bill Gates corner anyway. He was hearing plenty in his ears about it. All kinds of reports from the highest ends of the agencies that keep us protected from the things we have no idea is going on.

The next day Bill was standing on the steps of the federal court house. He left the reporters with, "We have reached an agreement." I'm not sure what else he could have said. The, what seemed to Shep to be, abrupt end to negotiations left room for conspiracy theory. Maybe Bill said "Look, give me something fair and I will not look for the human bugs you got this nanotechnology in." Something like that.

Shep knew this was possible but a far far cry from realistic. None the less he was pretty confident that the possibility of the nanobugs had now crossed Bill Gates mind. He would probably not want to get involved do to the impact it could have on the stability of our social wellbeing.

The fact Shep happened to be tuned in to something he watched few and far between, due to his constant meth movement, geeked up, goes to show that coincidences are cool. If I'm lying may the Recluses find me with that baseball bat. Two weeks later one of the news networks ran this across the bottom of the screen, and Shep read it four times, no doubt it was there.

++Two drug lords in Virginia acquitted due to a threat to national security++

Shep had let the idea of him being a human bug all but go. He would never know if Bill had found two people that were really human bugs. The court room falling in as a normal day. An attorney from Bill Gates sits unnoticed in the spectators section. His clue, a scanning of the airwaves from a device taken out of one of the Billionaires technology labs. Flying over a jail picking up a signal. Who was in the jail worth bugging, maybe the biggest drug lord or the addict. They go for the big guy? They would just listen more than likely. No need to talk to a human bug, less to experiment with persuasion.

Drug lords standing in front of the judge, and Bill's attorney pulls a frequency generator (scanner) from his pocket approaching the accused. Confirms the radio waves being transmitted. The DEA is there and would like to have a word with the judge who is already ordering them to his office. The news reporters have got a story but of course it's one that will never be fully told because it is a threat to national security.

Shep's greatest "What if it really happened?" is now via this book, on the table for contemplation of coincident or not coincident. The ones involved, beyond Shep, will be the only ones that ever know the truth, no matter how they tell the story.

Chapter 49

The computer voice of Shep's mind "2:46am" answers the agent, on a Bluetooth ear bud, at the cabin, sitting in a recliner playing Call of Duty on the large flat TV. "Good answer....Shep" The agent has a ear bud in his other ear to hear the game with out Shep hearing it. Shep knew nothing of the way the game sounded. If he heard it and connected it to be real, it would be his own undeniable proof he was in fact a human bug. Two other agents napped in recliners, another was on the internet waiting for their time to be on point.

Shep sat in darkness, faded by a night light, on the sofa at home, grandma's house to himself. Nothing but baggy shorts on his ass and a helmet of tin foil on his head. He was contemplating the agents response of "Good answer." as he moved a thin copper wire around to different contacts of a 9 volt walky-talky he had gutted. The wire passed through a rather large coil from a satellite TV dish. The wire continued to the foil helmet, weaving in and out tiny holes all around his head. The wire was then connected to the positive side of the 9 volt battery and terminal. He questioned the agent, in the course of meaningless conversation, by speaking out loud. It was heard over the room speakers at the cabin. "Good answer, good answer? Why you got to be a smartass? Why not just say thank you?" He never got over feeling strange when talking to them out loud when he was alone, so he seldom done it.

The agent pointed out, "Shep you know you could just think it, I get the impression somebody has acquired your company, and your talking to them, that being the case 99.9% of the time when we hear you over the room speaker. And it weird's me out picturing you sitting alone talking out loud."

"Me too." Shep disconnected the wire from the positive side and hooked it to the negative.

"Hold on Shep I'm being ambushed. Bap, bap, bap, mmm, mmm, bap, die mother fucker die mmm bap. OK Shep I'm still alive, I am Call of Duty hero. You may have thought, half past a monkeys ass quarter too it's balls. So in that respect you gave a good answer, you stupid fuck, I forgot to give you hell."

Shep just whispered with just breath no voice "You ain't from around here are ya'? You talk different."

"Shep, God Damn it they on me! NO! I am not from this HICK ASS STATE!"

Shep was taking his helmet off and it's connecting the wires, thinking how crazy he was playing Russian Rolette with a big ass coil and a 9 volt battery hooked to a electric chair cap, listening for a clue, some static or may be a high-pitched tone repeatedly in his ears, or a radio station would do it, he had way too much time on his hands.

The Yelling of the battle scared agent woke the other two up. One of them asked, "Hey, Shep, you fried your brain yet with that fucking gizmo you got there."

"No I gave up."

"Damn Shep I hate to hear that. I was hoping you would have smoke coming out your ears by now, so this mother fucker can pay me my money."

The agent playing the video game argued. "Shep, this stupid ass thinks that if you kill yourself with that satellite coil he wins the bet because you committed suicide. But that is accidental not suicide. He only gets paid for suicide. He is going to pay me when we are forced to shut down for any reason other than your death."

Shep smiled "Sometimes I don't know."

They all came alive. Kindling with, being up again at 3am looking crazy as hell. The fire grew to something bad happened stories, and every thing is Shep's fault.

Shep sat on his bed, boated up a foil and rolled with the punches.

"Shep, ALL YOU GOT to do man is stick your head in a microwave and it will block the signals."

"I already did"

" I know you did, and the only reason it did not stop us is because you did not shut the door, you got to shut the fucking door Shep."

"I am going to need a bigger microwave."

Chapter 50

Shep opened his eyes as the dusk till dawn camouflage truck eased off the shoulder of the road. It had been another night of cooking out in the woods with Stan on the other side of Twiggs County.

"A beautiful Sunday morning, I should have stayed in Cristal's driveway and slept a little longer, till she came to the door. I'll just pull off on the side of the road up here at the Asbwell's and take a power nap, they'll be going to church soon. Just ease it back on the road don't over react." These thoughts rushed through his head in a split second, as the ground fell from beneath the passenger side tires.

The gully the truck was falling in was falling off faster than he could pull it back on the road. The trees started slapping the passenger side mirror till it was torn off. Shep hit the gas to the floor and cut the wheels sharp trying to fishtail the rear around. Too late the truck crashed into a permanent oak at 65 mph., just right of dead center the Chevy bow tie.

Tail gate, back tires and all went up standing the truck on it's nose. Some how it ended up going between a forest of trees, bashing it's way to the bottom of the gully.

Shep was laying in the seat with four eight balls of meth in his pocket and a trash bag with two, one gallon cans of reusable toluene solvent and some meth caked coffee filters on the floor board. It all happened so fast after the permanent oak all Shep saw was a bright white light, then found himself in the bottom of a gully with the roof crushed in. The top of the windshield on the passenger side pushed out, catching Shep's right side shoulder. No seat belt.

The agents at the cabin sat in silence. Shep was thoughtless for a few till he regained his senses. "I'm alive."

They tore into him. "Shep you stupid son of a bitch, that's what you get!" "Yea, Shep I hope you broke your legs!"..........etc. etc.etc.

Shep gave it a thought, "Well, fuck you too." He tried to kick the door open, but ended up squeezing his body out the busted door window. Sliding out to his feet he felt the rush of surviving. Looking up at the fifty yards of steep hill to Hwy. 80, he did his best Ric Flair. "WHOOOOOO!" The crisp morning air and the smell of the woods was noticed. "Yea baby."

Tiffina tuned in and spoke at any time, expectantly when something was going down that was crazy. She was on speed dial. She tuned in just in time to hear, "Yea baby!" "Shep, Yea is right, but we don't say Yea baby. Got a call, said you just fucked up and might be hurt, what happen was it that damn deer, did that deer run out in front of you?"

Shep spoke in a whisper "No I kinda' nodded off."

"That makes you stupid! Could have killed somebody!"

The Recluses at the cabin and the others that had the bug phones started co-signing on her true statement. Shep signed it too, as he grabbed the trash bag with the cans and filters in it, going deeper in the woods. He stashed it and the half ounce behind a fallen tree , putting some leaves over it.

"It looks like I'm climbing out a hole once again." His shoulder and neck had some soreness setting in. Up on the Hwy. he continued for the west, with a slight limp. The Asbwell's just around the corner, a bit would be leaving for church any minute. He made it as they slowed at the end of their driveway. Mr. Asbwell a large jolly ordained Southern Baptist, let his window down as he and his wife waited for an explanation.

Shep told it with a hint of, I am just going to lie about this one. "What happened was I came around a curve back there and a deer met me head own. I was surprised at the sight of it running toward me in my lane I reacted by carefully easing off the side the road. Long story short my truck kissed a oak tree and it's in the bottom of that gully with no chance of revival. The deer, I suppose is round about Jeffersonville by now headed east on 80. It looked at me like it was in a big hurry as it went by my window."

Mrs. Asbwell found she wanted more. "Do tell."

Mr. Asbwell was not surprised. "That deer, that deer has done wrecked so many vehicles in this county, I hear the insurance companies have got a price on it's head."

That led to Shep calling the Sheriff Department being he had to call a truck to pull the truck from the gully and blocking the road was the only way. The Deputy was cool he looked at Shep's insurance card and pointed out it expired at midnight the night before. He then looked at the truck that was being pulled between trees and digging up dirt with front tires facing in opposite directions. Front bumper pushed to the engine and then some. Roof smashed half flat. He handed the insurance card back to Shep. "Good thing you won't be needing it."

Mama Jean came and picked him up and he decided, reluctantly, to go have x-rays, the vertebrate at the top of his back felt injured. During the x-rays a Recluses tapped the mute button and the five seconds of quiet had Shep's attention. He knew better and the Recluses went with it like this. "Shep, Shep the x-rays knocked the bugs loose you are cured!" "Yea Shep you can't hear us anymore." "Shep how dose it fell to be rid of the voices in your ears?"

On the way home Tiffina had an orgasm in the way Meg Ryan had in When Harry Met Sally. She like to make Shep feel embarrassed around certain people. Shep looked out the window at the scenery passing by, wanting to go with Tiffina but stuck with Mama Jean.

Mama Jean broke her silence. "You need to get your life together."

With Tiffina at the top of her solo, Shep did not disagree. "You don't know the half of it." The smile he foolishly tried to keep to himself was for the way his fucked up life had been everything and more than he expected, He was not sure if he magically had the opportunity to start it over if he would start over.

The voices, there to keep him aware of the non-stop conversation of what the fuck ever, had Shep put a stipulation on the start over. "If I knew y'all would go away some day real soon I would not start over. So I would start over because reaching my highest expectations would be cake with dog shit icing. So if I could escape this on the next go round I would go for it and hope to reach my dreams in some other way. I just can't imagine any thing else having the….." The entire time he was explaining his ears listened to them comment on his subjects with a wide range of personal reflection. "How much longer will I live if y'all stay?"

Chapter 51

Dell, the still looking like a kid, from Gailu dr. friend of Shep's stopped by in the A-Team van to check on Shep two days after the crash of the truck. He took Shep about 8 miles east on 80 to get his shit he hid in the woods. Shep paid him a half gram and a caked up filter for his troubles.

The day's with no transportation went by slow. The voice's seemed to be his center of attention, not that it was anything new, just more noticeable. When he could change his environment the subjets tended to be more colorful.

Half the meth sold the other half went up in smoke. Cristal had been dropped off and kept he company till the speed was gone, then she was gone, no surprise. Shep paid some of the bills with the money but didn't have enough for the entire tab. No meth, no ride, all his friends seemed to be disappeared.

He still had the Recluses. The bed was hard to leave some days. It would seem if he got up and did something it had to be better than thinking a never ending conversation with no environmental influence. Not his case, he was so drained it was just easier to lay there and think conversations that sounded somewhat like a kid fighting sleep just babbling to stay awake. He hoped they would get tired of him and leave. 30 days of it and no sign of that. Some times he hoped he die. They just never shut up.

His appetite was the first thing to come back. He would go eat over to his aunts. MaMo made him feel better, just because she was his grandmamma. She didn't seem to have any hard feeling about being evicted by Mama Jean and Shep making himself at home. On the table it was a ever so often meal, 15 bean soup and corn bread.

At the kitchen table Shep and MaMo talked the weather. Shep was trying to come up with something to say so MaMo would be entertained. Mama Jean was wiping the counter and putting dishes in the cabinet from the dish washer. Shep wondered if MaMo may have a few voices in her ear, giving her lately state of mind.

MaMo and Shep made eye contact. She winked at him and said "Fifteen bean soup, show clean ya' pipes."

Not what Shep wanted to hear coming from his MaMo's mouth, on account it instantly paints the picture of what is to come out the other end. The Agents jumped on it like stink on shit. The fart noises started along with, "Shep, Granny fixing to take a major dump." ....etc.

All Shep could come up with was, "Gee MaMo."

She slurped down the last spoon full of her soup then clinked her spoon in the bottom of the bowl. "But it do."

The voices. "Damn Shep, she said but it do. It do, dodo but." etc

Shep's funny bone was being tickled, he was biting his lip to control himself. It was out of character for her to say a thing of that nature. She excused herself from the table dropping her bowl in the sink she exited the kitchen.

"OOOO Shep, did she leave a silent one?"

Shep noticed Mama Jean seemed to be bighting her lip too, as she poured the left over soup in a storage bowl. She changed the subject. "Bout' time you found another job ain't it."

Shep knew it was coming and as obvious as his dilemma was she still made him explain. "I ain't got a ride now ya' know but I been trying to figure something out. I don't know what to do. They won't Shut up in my ears, I mean working is good cause it gives opportunity to multi-task. Even that gets to a point I just want to take a break."

"Just ignore them its all in your head."

Shep agreed. I know they are all in there. I don't know how many, and it's in my ears I hear them so ignoring them is impossible."

Sterling bug phoned in. "Shep I got one for ya'. Hey Recluses let me have the floor y'all take a break. Shep this is bad news man, Mama Jean confided in my mama, since my mama has been a nurse for forever. She asked her if she could give her a lead on a cancer doctor. Shep she has got it, but they caught it early. It's so small she don't want people worrying about it so she ain't told y'all. I just want you to know so when she dose tell you will know we are real. Don't you say….."

"Mama Jean, Sterling just said you got cancer." She was running a rag over the counter again, her face lost all expression the pause lasted long enough to be noticed. "Just don't listen to him." She continued to wipe the counter, again.

He put his bowl and stuff in the dishwasher, and put a arm around her shoulder. "Thank you for everything, I love you."

"I love you too."

Shep had one foot out the door being followed by a reminder.

"Get a job, I know you in a bind but ask your friends, maybe they could pick you up and take you to work."

Shep took the cancer thing with a grain of salt, "Mama Jean, Clean Jean, who never smoked, or drank, she been preaching at us kids for twenty years about it. I know that any body can get it but, Mama Jean will out live me, certainly at this rate."

Post note: We lost our Mama Jean to ovarian cancer after her six year fight to survive. She still lives as a strong inspiration in many ways of my life.

The Final Chapter 52

As I/Shep stated earlier, I do not know and can not account for the things that may have been going on I was not a witness to. This is just one of countless ways that the events may have unfolded. I chose to take this story into a science-fiction realm of mind reading with the voices staying real people because that's the way it played out in my world, even having no faith in their realness and (This reason came after I got done with a page of philosophical and psychological insight that was reworded and erased to explain in a different context way too many times.) This is the truth, as is my witness, in so many ways. It just made for a damn good book.

This much is true, Shep was sitting in his room, the window was up just a few inches, the blinds closed, covering the hole. He had a CD player that didn't work, so he was taking it apart to see why. Thanks to Stan stopping by the day before that, hooking him up with some meth to sell and some to do.

Them damn crickets, out there every night, every chirp a syllable of a endless circle in conversation. Shep often imagined himself standing over the voice masking lap top computer in a cabin smashing it with Shane's softball bat.

"Shep, Shep, Shep, you would only be smashing Tiffina. Dumbass has played that part the entire time.".........

Oh, let him count the times Shep considered it to be that way. He always instantly concluded it had to be a chick, no way was a man going to say, and sound like she did. He accepted that his brain had developed another human being, this one female, with no calibration of himself. He did not create her knowingly. Or he had a real chick talking to him on a bug phone.

Mean while, miles away, Sterling laid in his bed awake thinking about human bug and DEA stuff. A slight whisper so soft and quiet it seemed to be his brains voice. "Check on your mama." Rolling over to see the bright green digital clock numbers spelling out 1:38 a.m..

A few states away Scooter's in his lab coat inside the mountain. A microphone on the desk dialed into Sterling's frequency. Who he had bugged some time ago incase this time should ever arise. He had only performed a test from the human bug broadcast system, with the whisper.

The time had risen, due to the NSA contacting Scooter. They had been contacted by the Department of Defense. They had been contacted by Deryl's brother, Andy, his high security clearance and his quality of brains had some pull at the Air Force Base. Andy had been told by his Mama that she had cancer and how Shep was told by the voices in his ear.

Mama Jean was thinking about dieing. She knew the cancer was growing and they would try to stop it. Cutting out her ovaries, the next step. She had lived her life staying in the lanes, going the most logical way. She had a crazy thought and found herself laughing at it. She wanted to do something to help Shep in his human bug war. His heart was in the right place, for the most part.

Andy knew about the voices, along with the human bug theory. "Great theory" he said, "but since they are reading your mind that is all it will be, forever and long time." He knew the listening and talking to a human bug by simply putting some nanobugs in their food was not to far fetched, it would be here soon if not already.

Mama Jean knew Shep was not a human bug. The mind reading technology was just a bit much. Her and Andy discussed the possibility of human bugs being made and Andy pointed out the many negative effects it would have on the world. There is no stopping it but maybe if we saw it coming we could be prepared for it. He knew three people that would be interested in something like this. A high ranking Air Force man that was always talking about conspiracy in the government. A co-worker that was highly respected for his great contributions of technological genius, and was studying the field of nanotechnology. The lady he had in mind worked for the Department of Defense at one time. Andy got them to consider the possibilities by telling them about his cousin. For better results he left out the mind reading part. They took it to the next level, the Department of Defense.

The attention getter was a bluff. The technological guru said they knew with little doubt Shep was bugged and they were in the process of getting undeniable proof. Unless the voices stopped it was going to make world news. From the story Andy had told, they considered Shep possibly a human bug. Andy being the only one of them thinking the voices would never leave being his own mind reading his own mind.

Sterling would have been thinking he'd sound crazy as human bug if he went to calling his mom at near 2 a.m. because he was thinking out of no where something was wrong with her. He let the notion of himself being a human bug, in consideration of the thought that was almost a whisper, go with a, "Oh well.". He would send Shep down there to see if anything looked out of the ordinary. He got out of bed and keyed in with his bug phone. "Shep take your ass down to my mamas and see if her door is kicked in or any thing looks out of place like men running out the house, I don't know what your looking for, just walk down to that end of the street and back. I'm going back to bed. y'all call me if something ain't right."

Shep booted up and took off to scope it out. Figuring the back door would be the most likely point of entry he went the extra mile. He crossed Gailu dr. into his parents yard, still in Hawaii, to a field behind their house. Leading to a walk in that field behind the houses on that side of the street, till just before the house in question. At that point he entered woods, in that same step a dog started barking from a fenced in yard. Then seven joined in. Shep turned around it was obvious no one would be getting past all that racket with out raising the dead.

The next morning 10:35 a.m. Sterling backed out his new white Ford truck, blue stripe tag on the front, leaving home. Grey cloudy skies. He was headed for the cabin, after a stop by Wendy's to pick up some burger's for the gang of Recluse's.

As he sat with a hamburger list of variety in hand waiting to place his order, he was the only one in line, a familiar voice spoke in his ears. "You've got company." Sterling accepted the whisper from the night before as what it was. Then added this voice of Scooter to it and with no surprise he accepted he was a human bug. At this point an alien passing him on the interstate riding a unicycle would not surprise him.

Scooter was on his way down a corridor in the mountain going to the cafeteria. He had a bug phone to his face. "Sterling don't feel privileged. All human buggers get bugged. It's how I do it at the NSA. That's just to keep it fair, then again it really don't make sense. I don't know why I decided to start doing it. I can not hear you think and don't care what you got to say. Go shut Shep down."

Scooter decided it was time. The ones he had to answer to questioned weather it was a good idea for him to do what they had done to Shep in the first place. He got word in a round about way of a few of Shep's Human Bug War attacks. Starting with State Rep. Kenneth Birdsong, who Shep had called and spoke with. "I wouldn't doubt it one damn bit son. Put it in writing send it to me and I'll take it from there." Donald Rumsfeld and General Colin Powel, Shep did not talk to them but their secretaries. Bill Gates had done his part. .

Sterling saw no rush. Shep had put up with it a little shy of 4 years a few more minutes will only make him stronger. After he got the hamburgers the rain came slow to build a good steady pace.

Shep was at MaMo's in a recliner by the den sliding glass door wishing he could just hear the rain for 10 minutes with no other noise. The TV was on, he had his attention in conversation and looking at the job section of the paper for his lucky break. He had know idea a lucky break was fixing to find him. The voices carried on as usual constantly and they talked all the time non stop. Tiffina was hooked in and had a secret. She had got a call from Scooter advising her if she wanted to say good buy to Shep she needed to be in the conversation in the morning.

Sterling was in his truck at the cabin, rain blurred his widows. He contemplated on how to go about it. Not one for long good byes he grabbed the bag of burgers.

The agents in the cabin heard the Georgia Boots stomp twice across the porch and then door busted open.

Shep in the recliner in Dry Branch thinking there was a silence in the rain that he would like to hear. Tiffina commended him on it, saying it was some deep shit and that's why she liked him. The conversation of them mostly hollering about jobs for a few minutes gave way to ones telling Shep how he had went to college to be a lawyer and switched to criminal justice, got hired by the FBI and now he was CIA, "Never to late to…………….. change Shep," That's when Shep heard the door slam and orders started being called on. "I got the Beacon Cheese burger." "I got the double no cheese."

Sterling's voice next to the microphone, he was leaning into on the table, instead of picking the microphone up, he was loud and clear deep in Shep's ear. "You all got straight cheese burgers." Before any complaints came he continued. "SHEP, SHEP, SHEP, my man SHEP you going to be tuff enough man, I AM SHUTING THIS MOTHER FUCKER DOWN! THE NSA got me too and I ain't riding this train, I got to shut down!"

The agents assumed it was what Shep assumed. They said it was over with and all gave convincing bye's to Shep 5 to 10 times a month. "Yea Shep, we gone again." "Shep, fuck you I hope you OD on meth and I read about it in the paper soon!"

Tiffina let her secret go like she was fixing to pop. "I knew, I knew, SHEP, I knew since last night, buy Shep you make sure you make something out of this."

Sterling picked the lap top up with a micro phone hooked to it. "IT IS OVER!" He slammed the lap top on the floor and stomped on it with both boots a few times."

Scooter smiled and unplugged a cord from an electrical socket in his lab. It gave power to the computers that decoded all the conversions of mind to voice and voice to mind radio waves among other things.

Shep sat waiting for the talk, 5 seconds, 10, a minute he was still scared to believe it. From the kitchen he heard the refrigerator compressor start to hummm. The Recluses got in hummms like that and talked. Going through the kitchen to the breaker box he flipped the main, killing the power to every thing. The clock over the sink ticked its triumph as Shep walked by. He took the battery out just for good measure.

Laying back in the recliner he could not trust his brain just flipped the script like that. Trying not to think about them, trying not to concentrate on listening for them, trying to let them be gone for good. He multi-tasked, relaxing listening to the rain and letting the thought of the voices, potentially returning, simmer. 20 minutes and he not only heard the silence in the rain, between every drop just before it crashes, there is a silence, he also felt it. That feeling of peace didn't last but a few seconds. The worry of their return washed it away.

It's been over 10 years since that final bye. I/Shep have not heard any voices coming from that source, the Recluses aka my brain. Are they still in my brain talking to each other avoiding the neurological path ways of what is me. With 85 billion neurons in the brain, storing the chemicals that interact to be known as thinking, it gets complicated.

I had the ability to, for the most part, see things in a somewhat rational way. Meaning I did not go mass murdering people, no matter how real the voices sounded, even with the co-occurring going on in the real world that compounded the realness.

As for those who perceive life in a way it leads to such horrific extremes, it makes sense to them in some way. Well thought out or if the reason is chaos, that moment has became their destiny. How dose one make it to age 20+ and no one knew one day that person would go as far as mass murder. Of course it will happen. The debates of how far to go to try and stop as many as possible are too many and too much for the end of this book.

Voices in ones ears or mind are not needed for such extremes. What's more the extremes are not needed to find common ground in perception and reaction. We all have something that happens in-between perception and reaction that make each unique in some large to small way. Who are you?

I sometimes find myself thinking maybe there is a shadow of a possibility I was a human bug. Looking at the big picture, how they started and ended, all the convincing events in-between. BUT reading minds is not possible. That's how I know I was not a human bug.

I was busted and did about four years in the state pin for manufacturing meth, just about 6 months after the voices left. Had 10 years probation,, think I got about 3 left. I have been locked up about half the six years since my release for my inability to pass a piss test for the probation officer. I know it's only Rock n' Roll but I like it. That's what makes it something I don't want to stop doing but I have to. Or they will lock me up again and I hate jail.

I just lost the girl I have been with for 6 years because of meth, I had to try and beat them piss tests. Another year locked up in the state pin, so far she hasn't came back to stay, yet. I passed the last five piss test. Truth is I don't have to do meth in order to have a good day, I don't need it to get motivated, I love life with out it, and the kicker is I still wouldn't mind doing some. Because I like it. I hate I lost my girl Hanna. I hate jail it takes me away from my family. I'll stay clean today.

www.ingramcontent.com/pod-product-compliance
Lightning Source LLC
Chambersburg PA
CBHW062131280526
45788CB00001B/132